Stop Sweating & Start Talking

How to Make Sex Chats with Your Kids Easier Than You Think

Andrea Brand

WISE INK

ISBN 13: 978-1-63489-499-9

Library of Congress Catalog Number has been applied for.
Printed in the United States of America
First printing: 2021

25 24 23 22 21   5 4 3 2 1

Cover design by Zoe Norvell
Interior design by Patrick Maloney

Wise Ink Creative Publishing
807 Broadway St NE
Suite 46
Minneapolis, MN, 55413

To my family of origin
and the one I created with Alex

Contents

Introduction

"**S**o . . . have you talked to your kids about sex yet?"

This was the question I asked my friends on a crisp fall evening in 2012. I was hosting a dinner party that night for a half dozen couples who were all parents with kids around the same age. At that point, I was huddled with the women as we exchanged our latest parenting challenges. All of us had middle schoolers, so there was no shortage of topics being raised. And during a brief pause in the conversation, I asked how they were doing in the talking-about-sex department.

The looks of discomfort on their faces confirmed my suspicions. One of the women even blurted out, "Oh, THAT! I've been putting that conversation off." The nods, nervous murmurs, and lack of direct eye contact with me suggested she was not alone.

Not wanting to make any assumptions, I probed further. "Really? Is that true for anyone else?"

The answer was more or less the same for all of them. My public-health career had prepared me for this moment, and my curiosity was piqued.

Many of us plan to talk with our kids about sex, but how many of us actually follow through? We have good intentions, yet finding a point of conversation entry poses an irritating challenge for many people. If my friends—women who are smart, clued in, open, and easy to talk with—had difficulty broaching the subject, what was happening in other families? Surely they were not alone in feeling uncomfortable.

Admittedly, weaving subtle sex-education-related topics into conversations with my own two sons was not always as easy as I would have liked. But I persisted—if my husband and I didn't talk to them about such important matters and give them a foundation of accurate information, who would? Where would they turn when they had questions if they didn't know that we were a safe place for inquiry?

My involvement in the subject of sex education is longstanding. In college during the late 1980s, I was captivated by the human sexuality class, which introduced me to myriad aspects of sexual health that were new to me. This contributed to my participation in the formation of an on-campus peer-education program to impart information to students about safe sex, access to services, and overall sexual well-being. Around the same time, I obtained my first copy of *Our Bodies, Ourselves*, the ultimate guide on sexual health, empowering readers to take control of this part of their lives that historically was not discussed openly.

These collective experiences contributed to me packing my little hatchback and moving across the country to the

West Coast soon after college graduation to work in a women's reproductive health clinic. In this environment, I served women—young through middle-aged—and observed the degree to which a lack of information and misinformation are widespread. Simply put, receipt of factual sex education was not to be taken for granted.

Building on this experience, I returned to school to earn a couple master's degrees in social work and public health, allowing me to further my contribution to a field where I could marry my passion for reproductive health with my interpersonal skills. Now, more than twenty-five years later, my enthusiasm for and commitment to these areas has led me to this moment.

I was motivated to write this book for a number of reasons. First, I wanted to help parents make challenging sex conversations a thing of the past by opening the channels of communication and overcoming whatever fears get in the way. These talks can and will become easier and more comfortable. Imagine conversations about erections and sexual attraction that flow as easily as discussions about the forecast or the draft picks for your favorite sports team. Demystifying the subject of sex from an early age not only makes it more likely that kids will seek parents as a source of information but can help them talk more comfortably about sex with future partners and their own kids one day.

Second, I am passionate about arming youth with important information that promotes healthy and responsible behavior. The old adage *knowledge is power* is of particular relevance here, leading to greater self-esteem, stronger communication skills, and overall empowerment. One of the greatest gifts parents can give is accurate information that serves their children as they develop and become autonomous. A broad education about sex arms youth with important facts to live their best lives.

Finally, I wanted to share the model of a teen discussion group that I developed as a tool for parents to adapt and use on their own. I created the model (detailed in Part 3 of this book) out of a need for more sex-education opportunities that were comprehensive and comfortable, factual and fun. My experience of hosting a group ("Girls' Group" a.k.a. "GG") was impactful. The model lends itself to easily being replicated so that parents everywhere can help positively impact youth and future generations.

Anyone who is a parent or has observed friends or relatives who are parenting adolescents knows that this age group, with their developing prefrontal cortexes, will not always make the wisest choices. And that is beyond our control. What *is* within our control is the approachability and honesty with which we share information that will serve them.

This book is not a step-by-step solution with a verbatim script and timetable for conversations with your children.

Other books are available that focus on when to address topics at various stages in your child's journey. (I've listed some of my favorite resources in the Resources section.) Rather, this book, which is divided into three parts, offers tips and tricks to help you move beyond whatever is preventing you from opening up to your kids. Part 1 starts with background information about current sex education in the United States, why it needs to become more comprehensive and inclusive, and why it is important that you, as a parent, become more involved in your teen's sexucation (as 1 refer to it). Part 2 outlines my four-step process for helping you take on a more proactive role in your child's sex education by (in this exact order) getting in touch with your values about sex, learning which sex-ed topics are taught at your child's school, familiarizing yourself with available resources in your local community, and taking small steps to see big gains. Finally, Part 3 outlines the model 1 created for a sex education group, including suggestions for topics to cover and what factors you should consider if you want to form—or even facilitate—such a group.

My goal is to help you identify your roadblocks and devise ways to dismantle them so that you can talk with your kids with confidence. It might feel awkward at first, given that this is unfamiliar territory. But it will feel wonderfully rewarding too.

So what's getting in the way of having these conversations with your kids? And how can you overcome those obstacles? I can assure you that the concerns you have are surmountable and that talking to your teens about sex—believe it or not—is easier than you think.

Part One

WHAT YOU NEED TO KNOW ABOUT YOUR CHILD'S (LACK OF) SEX EDUCATION

Facts about Sex Education in the United States

How did you learn about sex? If you grew up in the 1970s and 1980s like I did, perhaps you found a book or pamphlet surreptitiously left on your bed from a conscientious but embarrassed parent. Depending on where you went to school, maybe you received a few lessons in biology or health (or "human ecology," as it was called in my Upstate New York suburban high school) that covered the physiological changes that happen to your body during puberty, with a very science-focused lesson or two that covered human reproduction. In brief, you might have officially learned very little beyond that adolescence includes acne, body odor, new hair growth, and gonadal changes, and the oversimplified formula that sperm plus egg equals baby.

Sound familiar? If your sex education even slightly resembled this description, it makes complete sense that you do not feel well equipped to have open, comfortable, and easy conversations with your own kids—you likely do not have a template from which to work. This describes the majority of us as we flail our way around trying to do what feels important without having a model to emulate. And for those of us who had a different experience altogether, some will feel less prepared for such conversations, while others will be more ready. Regardless, we all can benefit from overcoming what gets in the way of talking with our kids.

The US teen birth rate has been declining the last quarter century yet remains higher than in many other developed countries, including Canada and the United Kingdom.[1] Unfortunately, the rates of sexually transmitted infections among teens have not followed a similar trend. Those aged fifteen to twenty-four account for a quarter of the population yet make up nearly half of the twenty million new cases of STIs each year.[2] These stats are not meant to scare us parents. They are to motivate us. These numbers underscore that there is more—*a lot more*—we can do as parents and educators. There is plenty of room for us to improve what information we feed our kids so they are well informed with medically accurate facts. This will give them the tools to make healthy and informed decisions as they plod—or, in some cases, sprint—through adolescence and navigate their way toward adulthood.

School curricula have not consistently progressed from the decade in which you were in middle and high school. If you are hoping (with crossed fingers and toes) that your kid will learn all of the nitty-gritty details through a comprehensive sex education curriculum offered at school, that might very well be wishful thinking. Schools have the potential to be an amazing resource to provide our children with medically accurate, comprehensive, culturally sensitive, diverse sex education at developmentally appropriate intervals. And yet there are no national education standards by which states are required to abide. This means that there is an incredibly high level of variability regarding what, when, how, and if sex education is taught in school. States are left to determine their own requirements in this area.

As of February 2021, twenty-nine states and the District of Columbia require sex education to be taught in public schools. And get this: fifteen states do not require the curriculum to be medically accurate, culturally responsive, or evidence-based/evidence-informed. Let's pause here and allow that to sink in: only a subset of states *mandate* sex education in public school, and only a subset of those *require* it to be medically accurate. What does that mean in those states where medical accuracy is optional? How would you feel if your child's math, chemistry, or history classes were taught without a requirement that they be factual? Isn't the purpose of school to learn accurate information based on facts? And let's not forget that the remaining twenty-one states do not require any form of sex education in public school.[3]

For states that do impose sex-education requirements, there remain wide chasms regarding what topics are covered, the level of detail, and in some cases, the degree of scientific accuracy. YIKES. This sounds like it leaves a lot up to chance if we are relying on schools to educate our children about sex, sexuality, gender identity, birth control, reproduction, and the like. And by the way, *abstinence-only education is required in eleven states.*

If you live in a state where the minimum set of requirements is taught, inconsistencies still prevail. Local school districts within a state have a great deal of autonomy to meet the minimum requirements as they wish. This invites tremendous variability, inconsistency, and potential for misinformation. Additionally, school districts within the same state, even in adjacent towns, may rely on dramatically different curricula, if they use them at all, to guide them in what is taught to students. How does this guarantee that what is offered provides a solid foundation for the future?

So if schools are not a reliable source of sex education, who is? Where are kids getting their information? Parents and guardians are *hopefully* talking with their children, starting at a young age. Numerous small conversations throughout a child's development are the way to address this. And who is better equipped to offer information than a trusted parent who, while chatting, can weave their family's values into the conversation? This is true even if a school district offers sexuality education. Parents have an amazing opportunity to be at the center of their children's sexuality education. Simple as this might sound, this is challenging. Many of us start to hyperventilate at the mere thought.

When kids are not getting the facts they need in a developmentally appropriate manner at school, and when parents become tongue-tied every time they attempt to broach a topic related to sex, where does that leave our children? If we do not offer kids the sex education they deserve, we are basically telling them to figure it out on their own. I've known many teens in my lifetime, and I've learned that hoping they will learn something important without their parents giving them the necessary tools to support their learning is not a recipe for success.

I'll let you in on a little secret: you're not alone in feeling that it is difficult to talk to your kids about sex—to the point that your stomach becomes a ball of knots. This book will help you overcome those immobilizing fears and open the channels of communication in a manner that feels comfortable and right for you.

You Are in Good Company

So many parents wish they could talk with their kids about such important, natural life matters but feel blocked or don't know where to begin. And when we reflect back on our own upbringings, coupled with the hang-ups that many of us carry, it makes sense that conversation starters on this topic don't roll off our tongues.

If you were to take a cross section of parents who struggle with talking about sex with their children, you would see it cuts across all demographics: race, socioeconomics, religious affiliation, political views, geographic location, and more. In other words, this is not an issue unique to a small subset of parents within specific demographic categories. In fact, like sports fans rooting for their local celebrity team, we are a diverse group by any measure. My objective is to unify us parents as a team that is comfortable talking with our kids throughout their youth. Let's go, team!

It is perfectly normal to be challenged in this area, which is what led me to help other parents and guardians. This concern extends beyond the family unit. A few years ago, I had a driveway moment, staying in the car after arriving home to finish listening to something on the radio. In this case, it was a news story that described the conflict some doctors were experiencing when addressing specific health issues with adolescent patients and their parents. The story focused on a study that examined pediatricians and family physician practices regarding the human papillomavirus (HPV) vaccine, which became available in 2006 and is recommended as a routine vaccination for kids around age twelve.

The news story reported that many physicians do not proactively recommend the HPV vaccine to adolescents despite the vaccine's well-documented reputation as being safe and highly effective in the prevention of the most common strands that are known to cause certain cancers. Additionally, many doctors do not educate adolescent patients and their parents about the importance of the HPV vaccine because they are concerned that parents may feel it will encourage sexual activity. This is the same reason that often interferes with parents and schools addressing sex education head-on. Adults in this camp are concerned that talking about sexuality and sharing important factual information would give their young audience permission to become sexually active. In other words, they are worried about the power of suggestion.

DID YOU KNOW?

HPV is spread through sexual contact, and most cervical cancer is associated with particular strains of HPV. The incidence of cervical cancer can be largely prevented when the HPV vaccine is given before exposure to the virus. For this reason, the CDC recommends the HPV vaccine be administered to girls and boys (the latter of whom can be transmitters of the virus) around age eleven to twelve as a protection against cervical cancer later in a female's life.

Good news, though: there is no correlation between sex ed and earlier engagement in sexual behaviors. In other words, sex education does not encourage sexual activity in our kids. In fact, numerous studies have indicated the opposite, finding that comprehensive sex education is more effective than abstinence-only education across a number of measures.[4]

What does it tell us if doctors are also struggling with having open, honest, proactive talks with their adolescent patients? We rely on the medical community not only to treat us when we are sick but also to help us remain healthy. Dentists remind us about good tooth-brushing and flossing habits to prevent cavities and maintain oral health, while dermatologists drive home the importance of applying sunscreen to prevent skin cancer. Why, then, do some physicians avoid public health messages that center around preventative behaviors to maintain sexual health?

That's why I am here: to help you fill in the educational gaps that exist to encourage intentional, healthy behaviors.

Shifting from Rift to Gift

Curiosity is normal. Humans are lifelong learners. And curiosity about sex is a natural part of development that lasts a long time—almost the entire life span, in fact. The complicating factor is that this curiosity might be wrapped in shame for some inquisitive minds, based on cues picked up along the way from their families, schools, or places of worship. How liberating would it be if kids felt they could ask their parents ANYTHING without concerns of embarrassment, judgment, or penalty? How would it feel for you to be at ease with your kids' questions about sex without skirting around them, ending the conversation curtly, responding with untruths out of fear, or ignoring the questions altogether? Close your eyes and imagine that right now. It feels a lot better, doesn't it?

If kids are not getting information or sufficient responses from their parents, the curiosity does not magically evaporate. They will look for answers beyond the family bubble. They will talk with their friends who have heard, read, or seen things, perhaps from older siblings, who add a degree of perceived credibility, rightly or wrongly. After all, if the idolized older sibling of a friend said so, why would there be any reason to question it?

If you recall your own experience when you were growing up, you may remember that these second- and third-hand sources of information are not always accurate. One day when I was about seven years old, I was playing outside with one of my neighbors, who was a few years older than me. As we played with rocks and sticks, she nonchalantly explained to me that a girl gets pregnant when a boy puts a pebble in her vagina and it grows into a baby. Never one to

23

be shy, I proudly declared my new understanding of how babies were made to my family at dinner that evening. Immediately I knew something was amiss when my older brother, a young teenager, erupted with laughter. Meanwhile, my mother tried to disguise her dismay through her noble attempt at a poker face. And that was it. End of discussion.

Kids may—make that WILL—turn to unreliable sources of information to learn about sex in the absence of factual explanations. The problem is, they do not know that their source of information is unreliable, making it a perfect storm for becoming misinformed. The internet is the go-to source of information for many kids, largely because it is so accessible and private. Curiosity, coupled with embarrassment, makes the internet seem like an ideal solution. However, the internet offers access to much more than we bargain for and can send people with innocent queries to shocking sources. Imagine what results might pop up on the computer screen when a curious child looks up a term they heard on the playground or school bus.

This, my friend, is where you can make a difference. As a parent, you are perfectly positioned to be an amazing resource to your beloved children. You want only the best for them. And yet, like so many other parents, maybe you make the exception when it comes to open conversations about sexucation.

Before my first child was born, I consumed book after

book about babies' development that influenced my behaviors to feel a sense of control over the little human I was growing. I researched every gadget and gizmo that would become part of our daily routine before buying it. Car seat, stroller, diapers, baby hygiene products, bottles, crib sheets, mobiles, pacifiers, exposure to music, tummy time. Every purchase and every decision was made with careful calculation and deliberation. I was doing everything I could imagine to ensure the health and well-being of the little nugget, including how I took care of myself during the pregnancy—nutrition, exercise, sleep—for optimal baby development. And once he arrived, the pattern continued. Admittedly, the "have to do this or he'll be negatively impacted" attitude relaxed as my confidence in parenting increased, and yet his health and development still informed many of my actions. How much does this resonate with you?

With this in mind, how is it that we find ourselves devoting an inordinate amount of time dwelling on small and often inconsequential decisions and tossing aside others with real and long-lasting impact? Many parents find themselves overthinking such decisions that, in the end, do not truly matter. In contrast, some of us find ourselves barely acknowledging the provision of critically useful life skills. I am referring to information about independent survival such as cooking, budgeting, map reading, contraception, mutual consent, wilderness safety, house repairs, etc., etc., etc.; in other words, those things that will *actually* serve kids over the course of their lives.

Think about what you stand to gain by talking with your kids about sex. From this, you can reap a whole host of benefits: prevention of unintended life events, maintenance of good health, acceptance and inclusion, and trust between you and your child, just to name a few. What is the cost? The initial discomfort of talking about sex, which will hopefully be lessened after you finish reading this book. So what do you stand to lose by NOT having these conversations with your kids? In other words, what are the more likely outcomes of avoidance? Without a solid foundation of accurate information, your kids may seek answers from unreliable sources and potentially experience greater associated health risks simply out of ignorance—ignorance that is completely avoidable. They may also miss the opportunity to develop the values you hold deeply and want to share with them.

We parents love our kids, and we want them to be healthy, happy, kind, contributing humans. Our role as parents and caregivers is to keep them safe and provide them with love, basic necessities, and support so they grow to reach their potential. Conversations about sex and comprehensive education on the topic are a part of this. Together, we can normalize conversations about sex so that our fears around it become part of an old story—*your* old story—that is no longer applicable. This might sound scary, but you are here, taking the first step toward working through that fear.

So congratulations! You are on your way to making the discomfort of difficult conversations a thing of the past. This book shares the eye-opening reality of current (mis)information that reaches your kids, as well as proactive and responsive actions you can take to be a positive influence.

❋ 2 ❋

Sexual Content Is Everywhere

Your ability (or inability) to talk with your kids about sex doesn't change the fact that we all are surrounded by sexual messages that are subtle or blatant. You can bury your head in the sand, turn a blind eye, or tune out as much as you want. But sexual content is ubiquitous, and it is reaching your kids. Let's go over some of those sources.

Pornography

The current ease of access to porn is a far cry from my experience as a sixteen-year-old in the 1980s when I accompanied my bold friend who volunteered to rent a graphic X-rated video for a pizza gathering for our group of six girlfriends. We were curious to see what this porno stuff was all about. And let me say, I was in for a big surprise. If only we had a camera recording everyone's reactions. Our wide eyes and gaping mouths expressed shock, disgust, and delight as the camera zoomed within inches of body parts engaged in sexual intimacy. And all this explicit entertainment appeared within two minutes of pressing play. The directors wasted no time building a plot. They cut right to the chase, or so the saying goes.

Wow, was I naive.

People are drawn to sex. By nature, the majority of humans are sexual, curious beings. The enormous porn film industry is one indicator of this. The big dollars spent here indicate that there is a big market for pornography. The great demand for pornography is fueled by consumers' hunger for sex. The industry would not survive, let alone thrive, without such demand. People from varied socioeconomic backgrounds, races, religions, gender identities, and sexual orientations watch porn, if not regularly then at some point in their lives. About forty million Americans are regular viewers of internet porn, and the average age at which a child first sees online porn is eleven years old. This does not mean kids are regular visitors or are even intentionally searching for it.[5] In fact, 34 percent of internet users have accessed porn unintentionally through misdirected links, email, and pop-up ads.[6]

Well-researched scholarly articles and entire books address the great porn debate well beyond the objectives of this book. For our purposes, let's acknowledge the indisputable fact that pornography holds a huge piece of the internet marketplace—and this has implications for people of all ages. The amount of money spent on producing and selling porn is difficult to measure for a number of reasons. Many porn businesses are privately held; therefore, the revenue they generate is unknown. Additionally, there is a significant piracy market—unauthorized duplications of porn videos are sold at a lower cost—that exists and is not factored into the industry's bottom line. These factors contribute to miscalculations of the true gross income of the porn industry. By all accounts, the amount of money consumers spend on porn may be significantly underestimated.

And given the great demand for it, porn is easily accessible. In the pre-internet days, movie rentals from the local video store and magazines such as *Playboy*, *Penthouse*, and *Hustler* were the go-to sources for satisfying one's hunger for sexual content. One risked embarrassment when renting or purchasing such a publication at the store or newsstand if they did not have access through friends or a family member's hidden stash. Today it is a different story altogether. Access to porn is literally at the fingertips of anyone with a computer or smartphone. The increased "convenience" factor is a double-edged sword. Individuals (such as youth) who are ill-prepared to comprehend all of the issues regarding what appears on their screen can access it as easily as others who have a more mature understanding of what they are watching. Even animated porn, which is created in a format similar to *Family Guy* and *The Simpsons*, is a thing! This is a perfect example of providing subject matter intended for mature audiences in a kid-friendly format.

How would you feel if you learned your child was watching porn? How would your opinion change if they had yet to receive sex education? Imagine that your child's first exposure to sex is through a porn site, so it's strictly visual and auditory but without a voice-over that explains what is happening or why. This can be a frightening and unforgettable introduction for someone who doesn't have the knowledge or emotional tools to comprehend what she is watching (and even for some more mature viewers who do have such tools). A kid's first exposure to porn, in the absence of any formal sex education at home, at school, or in a community organization, may serve as a quasi sex-ed tool by default. Scary thought, isn't it? If it feels that way for you, let me assure you that your kid is neither the first nor the last to actively seek out or accidentally stumble upon porn sites on their phone or computer.

There is a dearth of resources that help parents navigate their children's natural curiosity, given porn's accessibility. One book that deserves mention is Cindy Pierce's *Sexploitation: Helping Kids Develop Healthy Sexuality in a Porn-Driven World,* listed in the Resources section at the end of this book. A couple of tips for you:

- Proactively talk to your kids in ways they understand about online safety and healthy sexuality, boundaries, and consent.

- Create rules and parameters about internet use for young kids that you can modify as they get older. They may be more tech savvy than you, but they still need and actually prefer to have parameters from you around the good and bad of the online world.

- For younger kids, use concrete, specific statements such as, "If you ever stumble upon something where you see naked private parts, come tell me. If that happens, you've done nothing wrong and you are not in trouble."

- As they get older, more details about why you do not want your child watching porn are appropriate. Portrayals of a lack of conversation between partners, aggression and violence during intimacy, and body representations are useful to discuss in the context of mutually consensual, healthy relationships. A letter I wrote to my son addressing these issues can be found in Chapter 7.

**PARENTAL CHALLENGE: Comparing Your
Childhood Resources with Those Today**

What kinds of questions did you have about your changing
body during puberty? Imagine what happens today when a
boy's confusion about spontaneous erections leads him to an
innocently curious search on the internet. What search terms
would he use? ("Erections"? "Erection in school"? "Erection in
sleep"?) More importantly, what websites and images would it
lead him to?

Romance Novels

During the 1980s, when I was a tween/teen, my peers and
I ravenously read books by Danielle Steel and Judy Blume
in search of descriptive and steamy sex scenes. These au-
thors offered private access to information about romance
and sex that went well beyond what our parents taught us—
that is, *if* our parents talked to us about it—and what we had
learned in health class at school. This was particularly true
for the many twelve-year-olds who read passages of *Forever*
aloud to each other at sleepovers and overnight summer
camp when we got ahold of our counselor's dog-eared copy
that made the rounds around the bunks. As one friend mentioned, Judy Blume's *Forever* was her source of sex education
at sleepaway camp.

Saucy romantic novels have been a popular genre of

fiction for decades. Remember Harlequin romance books? These were popular when I was growing up. Though they were not my preferred genre for reading, I'll never forget the dramatic covers that showed bare-chested, muscular men in a heroic pose while staring deeply into the eyes of a modelesque woman. This is where the long-maned model Fabio rose to stardom—or at least where I first observed him on displays while I waited in the supermarket check-out line—having graced more than 450 book covers.[7] The demand for romance novels is still huge today. In fact, romance is a billion-dollar industry annually, accounting for somewhere between one fifth and one third of adult fiction sales.[8]

Erotic fiction, or erotica, is a subgenre of romance novel that is typically more liberal and graphic regarding sexual content. E. L. James's *Fifty Shades of Grey* found unprecedented success after it was published in 2011. By 2017, the trilogy had sold over thirty-five million copies in the United States, with the first installment becoming the best-selling book of the decade.[9] With the popularity of e-readers and online booksellers such as Amazon and Barnes & Noble, curious consumers too shy to purchase or borrow a book in person can discreetly get their fill of erotica without venturing out in public. Additionally, a plethora of websites allow anyone to post and read erotic short stories for those interested in smaller bites to get their fix.

Budding romance and steamy scenes sell, even without the confines of any significant plot. Many curious adolescents and prepubescents experience increased curiosity for romance and erotic literature. Such writings offer detailed descriptions that allow imaginations to run wild. To a youngster, it can be both fascinating and cringeworthy. And whether one reads with hungry eagerness or trepidation, the demand for literature of this genre remains steadily high, as evidenced by its sales.

Whether you are a frequent consumer of this type of literature, have read a few pieces of work in this category, or have never turned a single page, you can probably guess which parts of a romantic or sex scene are emphasized and which ones are left out. As romantic seduction builds and the characters' passion for each other practically leaps off the page, have you ever observed a protagonist pause to say something like "Excuse me while I fetch a condom" or "The dental dam is in the drawer of the bedside table"? Remember, sex sells. Increased sales of these books are correlated with their level of steaminess, not with their discussion of which birth control method to use. But when discussions of safe sex practices are excluded from romance scenes in books—or any medium, for that matter—it is a disservice to readers who have yet to receive sex education and are unable to recognize their absence.

Advertisements and Media Literacy

Have you ever driven along the highway and observed a billboard displaying an attractive woman in a seductive pose with a headline that you may not have had time to read before it was out of view? Chances are you have, without ever realizing what product was being advertised in that giant photo on the side of the road. And that's the point. Images of scantily clad, provocative women (often girls) are frequently used to promote products that have nothing to do with the models staring down at us while we cruise past at sixty-five miles per hour.

Back in the mid-1980s, I took a marketing and advertising class in high school. At one point, we watched *Killing Us Softly*, the debut film by activist and brilliant media-literacy expert Jean Kilbourne. During the movie, she gently walked the viewer (with appropriate, humorous interjections as needed) through the process in which female images are altered and used in advertising. My mind was moving at high speed after I watched how blatant and subtle images of women's and girls' sexuality were being used to sell products of all types. Suggestive poses and sexual innuendos were incorporated into ads for everyday products—from fashion, perfumes, and cosmetics to beer and cars—in an attempt to create appeal and desire for the lifestyles represented in the ads. Once you see it, it's almost impossible to unsee it—and believe me, it's everywhere.

The advertising industry's use of sex to sell products is a tried-and-true trick that has been in place for decades. We can find this imagery in everything from the billboards that line our municipal highways to magazine and TV ads. Suggestive pictures of beautiful people clad in minimal clothing lure prospective consumers to buy or use products. It's geared toward making you think, *Hell, if using that product will make me look that young, thin, sexy, etc. and have that kind of lifestyle, sign me up. I want to be like them—and if I buy that product, I will be like them.* This is precisely how advertisers hope prospective consumers will think. And for viewers who lack media literacy (and that's many of us), the public-health implications—low self-esteem, body image concerns, eating disorders, depression, anxiety, and much more—are real and significant.

DID YOU KNOW?
Media literacy is the ability to use critical thinking skills to decipher the messages and symbols used by advertisers.

Since the original release of *Killing Us Softly*, Kilbourne has released three updated versions and continues to be a public speaker and media-literacy promoter. If you're not familiar with her work, I highly recommend checking it out. And if you think it's appropriate for your children, depending on their age and level of maturity, consider watching *Killing Us Softly* with them as an opportunity to open channels of communication on this topic. Media literacy is not routinely taught in schools around the country. Yet it is so important, given its connection to many public health concerns that are the result of unrealistic portrayals of people's bodies, the sexualization of young girls, and the like. A quick internet search for the film or Jean Kilbourne will lead you to a variety of useful resources including discussion questions that can serve as prompts for broaching this subject with your children.

Television and Movies

Television shows and movies come with TV parental guidelines, which are ratings that can be helpful for parents who question how appropriate a particular film or program is for their child. The rating system offers categories for minimum suggested age as well as content descriptors for suggestive or crude language, sexual themes, and violence. However, keep in mind that no one knows your child better than you do, so these ratings are *suggested* guidelines. For better or worse, should you choose to follow them or some modified version of such guidelines, it requires a degree of supervision by you, which you may or may not feel comfortable managing. This can feel like helicoptering to some parents.

Your parenting style is uniquely yours, and you want to trust it. It is not my intention to tell you how to parent your child or insist you follow a strict set of guidelines about what is okay for your child to view at what age. That requires an assessment that you are perfectly situated to make, based on your child's personality, maturity level, and developmental stage, and your own personal values. Rather, my intention here is to raise your awareness by getting you thinking about what your kids might be watching without your knowledge, if that matters to you. You are in a position to make an informed decision based on what feels right for your family. Many parents are unaware of the adult-themed programming that's available on television, which can be easily accessed through the generous and competitive cable TV/internet streaming packages that are now so common in households across the United States. Some will allow you to set parental controls, so you may want to explore that if it's important to you. But let's be real here: kids' access to television and movies goes beyond what they can click on using the remote control. Even if you choose to set parental controls, kids who are interested will likely find other avenues to access the forbidden fruit.

Music and Lyric Content

When I was growing up, I was fortunate to have an inexpensive turntable and speakers in my bedroom, so I would listen to LPs behind closed doors to tune out the world and get lost in my thoughts. I even saved my babysitting money to buy a knockoff version of a Sony Walkman on a field trip to New York City's Lower East Side. I could listen to cassettes for hours and hours on my bed through those spongy headphones. The too-loud music blocked out the household noise and spoke directly to me. The music vibrated throughout my body, and the messages resonated as if written for me. Oh, the ego of a fourteen-year-old!

Today, with many kids playing music through their smartphones via headsets, I smile at the rite of passage that is getting lost in the lyrics and discovering oneself through music. I am nostalgic for the days when music moved me so much as I identified with the lyrics of the painful journey of the singer as only a teen experiencing common adolescent angst can. However, now the stakes feel greater given the explicit nature of some of today's popular music.

Admittedly, I am a product of the 1970s music era, and it remains my go-to decade when I am looking to unwind with a trip down memory lane. My preferences aside, I've discovered that a great way to connect with my kids is through music. Sure, I exposed them to my music tastes when they were young, but now I try to meet them where they are and, at a minimum, listen to and try to learn what they enjoy about their playlists. Much of the popular music they listen to is stuff I enjoy too. And, of course, a sense of pride washes over me when artists from my past—the Beatles, the Eagles, and Queen, to name a few—are part of their repertoire. There is more overlap in our music tastes than there is disparity.

Then there is the *other* music my kids like. Without identifying specific artists or dissing anyone's musical preferences, I'll say that one genre of music is highly explicit and wildly popular among youth and adults alike. Though it is not for me, this style of music is unquestionably a display of amazing talent. In fact, many of these artists are Grammy winners and nominees, an indication of just how gifted they are.

In the 1980s, the Parental Advisory Label (PAL) was created for a handful of albums that were deemed "porn rock." This became a divisive issue as artists argued for freedom of expression and parents behind the labeling policy held the view that suggestive lyrics would negatively influence their malleable children's behavior. Now, with a vast majority of music being streamed rather than purchased in a format one can hold in their hand, the labeling has become almost a moot point. In all likelihood, your child is listening to explicit music. This includes every four-letter word imaginable, the n-word, dark and violent messages, and offensive references to sex.

Some, if not all, of the music your child is listening to will vary from your own playlist. This translates into an incredible opportunity for you to connect with your child through music. How can you engage your kids from a place of curiosity?

Even though I do not like some of the music my kids choose to listen to, I see their music choices as part of their development. It is an expression of their figuring out who they are. I can simultaneously dislike some of their music choices and love that they are able to appreciate various music styles. We have had many discussions about the meanings of songs, including those that I describe as angry soapbox rhetoric. What an amazing opportunity to communicate my values while they are discovering theirs. Our musical tastes overlap maybe 70–80 percent of the time. For the remaining 20–30 percent of the time, I embrace the opportunity to understand what they find appealing about music that does not resonate with me. And they have taught me a great deal.

There is a lot to be gained from these kinds of conversations with your kids. Discovering where music preferences are aligned and where they stray lends itself to interesting discussions with your children. An added benefit is the mutual sharing of thoughts and feelings that music provokes. Remaining open and nonjudgmental reinforces you as a trusted person and sets the stage for future conversations about a wide variety of subjects.

PARENTAL CHALLENGE: Taking Steps to Connect with Your Child through Music

These six steps may help you get to know more about your child. By staying curious, you are more likely to encourage openness in sharing:

1. Become familiar with what music your child is listening to. How can you do this? Here are some suggestions: Invite them to play their music in the car or at home when you are together. Ask them who their favorite artists are and why. Have them explain what they like about their favorites.

2. Use the content as an opportunity to raise issues important to you without shaming your child for liking the music.

3. Acknowledge that musical brilliance and offensive language/messages are not mutually exclusive.

4. Be honest about why you like or don't like the music without insulting your child's tastes.

5. Share that music preferences vary person to person and may change over time, and there is no right or wrong about our taste for music.

6. Express appreciation to your child for participating in open conversations.

* 3 *

The Need for Comprehensive
Sex Ed for Kids

Sex education does not come in a one-size-fits-all model, and its curricula vary tremendously from school district to school district. What this means is that the information included in lesson plans will vary across several measures, including what specific topics are covered, the degree of factual and medical accuracy, and the recognition of the amazing diversity of our population. When done thoroughly, sex ed helps teens navigate a crucial part of their identity and empowers them to make informed, intentional decisions about their sexual health.

Offering sex education in a school district is not simply a checkbox item. As we discussed earlier, schools apply this term loosely, with no consistent definition of what it encompasses. First, it is important to determine if sex education is included in the curriculum. Then, we have to assess the degree to which the curriculum is factual and medically accurate and covers the full range of topics that fall under this rubric. In other words, is it comprehensive?

What Is Comprehensive Sex Education?

The abstinence-only vs. comprehensive sex education argument is longstanding, and each camp feels deeply rooted on whichever side they stand. Many scholarly research articles point to strong evidence that makes the case for comprehensive sex education. Additional research points to the majority of Americans supporting comprehensive sex education for their children. And yet, fears and misconceptions of decision-makers, and money from influential groups, continue to perpetuate the use of abstinence-only programs in schools throughout the country.

In this time of stretched budgets within local governments and public school systems, money offered to promote abstinence-only education can sound more appealing. In recent years, federal funding has favored the promotion of this type of sex ed. In fact, millions of dollars have been thrown at abstinence-only programs in public schools. This limits what can and cannot be taught by institutions that are receiving federal monies through state Title V grants or directly through another federal funding mechanism that goes directly to community-based organizations.

A few years ago, a small town in western Texas made headlines because the local high school was reported to have an outbreak of chlamydia cases. Incidentally, this school does not offer any sex education. Texas requires sex ed to be abstinence-only, and the school bowed out of offering any information at all. This raises an important issue that historically has brought out strong opinions on both sides: What, if anything, should be taught in a school district's sex-education curriculum? What can be done to prevent the spread of sexually transmitted infections (STIs)? Clearly, neglecting to educate teens about what STIs are and how they can be prevented leads to practices that will continue to create new cases of chlamydia and other STIs.

Because Texas schools use an abstinence-only curriculum, the message students are receiving is that abstaining from sex is the only way to prevent unintended consequences, and they are not taught about condoms or other forms of protection and birth control. While it is hard for us parents to think about our kids ever being sexual, especially in the absence of marriage, I have a news flash for you: *teens are sexual beings, and that is perfectly normal and healthy*. You can either bury your head in the sand to convince yourself otherwise, or you can acknowledge that teens are sexual beings and likely to explore this aspect of themselves whether they receive sex education or not.

Research has reliably proven that comprehensive sex ed has many positive impacts. And yet there remain common myths related to sex education. Here are four of them:

MYTH #1: Comprehensive Sex Education in Schools Encourages Sexual Activity

FACT: Research supports that comprehensive programs contribute to delayed initiation of sexual intercourse, decreased frequency of sexual intercourse, decreased number of sexual partners, and increased use of contraception.[10]

MYTH #2: Abstinence-Based Sex Education Reduces the Rates of Teen Pregnancy and STIs

FACT: Many studies, including those overseen by the Centers for Disease Control and Prevention (CDC), support the finding that abstinence-only curricula do not reduce the rates of teen pregnancy or STIs. Several evidence-based comprehensive health-education programs (i.e., those that promote abstinence while also providing factual information about contraception and STI prevention) have proven to have greater effectiveness in this regard. However, there remains a strong misconception by many Americans that providing developmentally appropriate, accurate information will increase sexual behaviors among teens. Unfortunately, school districts that take this stance are missing an important opportunity to impart factual information to teens, rationalizing that avoiding the discussion will prevent them from engaging in risky behaviors. This hush-hush approach is not grounded in research and does not offer protection to teenagers who do not heed their lessons in abstinence.

MYTH #3: Sex Education Offered at School Lets Parents Off the Hook from Talking with Their Children about Such Topics

FACT: A comprehensive sex-education program is a wonderful addition to conversations you have with your child. But it should not replace opportunities to talk with your child to reinforce what they learn in school with the addition of your values woven into the content.

MYTH #4: Avoiding All Sex Talks or Education with Kids Is the Best Way to Keep Them from Getting Any Ideas about Sex

FACT: Teens are sexual beings, and pretending otherwise by ignoring this fact will put them at risk for engaging in risky behaviors. Having open, honest conversations and multiple learning opportunities does not make them engage in behaviors they otherwise would not. Instead, it gives them important information that will help them stay safe.

DID YOU KNOW?

Abstinence-only sex education emphasizes the importance of abstaining from sex until marriage. It does not describe the various barrier and hormonal contraception methods or discuss how to prevent sexually transmitted infections outside of abstinence. It is solely focused on male–female relationships, thereby disenfranchising other sexual orientations and gender identities. Meanwhile, comprehensive sex education conveys medically accurate information that includes significant discussion of abstinence as well as thorough coverage of contraception, STI prevention, healthy relationships, sexual identity, gender identity and expression, communication skills, consent, sexual harassment, and other related topics. It is inclusive of all groups.

Ultimately, comprehensive sex education gives young people thorough information about sex and sexuality so they can make the best, most informed decisions for themselves. This also means including abstinence in a sex-education curriculum and ensuring it is part of the full picture that is presented to students. When abstinence is promoted exclusively without putting it into a broader context, it has repeatedly been proven to be an ineffective sex-education strategy. But, as numerous studies have shown, when abstinence is one component of a larger discussion, it is much more useful. Preaching abstinence exclusively is similar to using scare tactics or shaming students into feeling that any other way is wrong. It is a fear-based approach designed to lead to avoidance behavior, but—for better or worse—it is not an effective strategy.

The Importance of Inclusivity

Gender and Sexual Identities

Up to this point, you may have grasped the main differences between abstinence-only curricula and comprehensive sex education. Other distinctions between these two general categories of sex education are important to raise. One limitation to highlight is that the majority of sexuality education is heavily heteronormative. (In other words, it assumes a heterosexual orientation.) While the majority of the population is heterosexual, it is irresponsible to leave out sex education that speaks to all sexual orientations, gender identities, and expressions.

Inclusive sex ed incorporates positive examples of LGBTQ+ individuals, couples, and families and emphasizes the need for safe sex practices for all people. It also shatters myths and stereotypes that perpetuate prejudice and bullying. But guess what? Only eleven states have sex-ed policies or discussion of sexual health for LGBTQ+ youth. And as of March 2020, six states—Alabama, Louisiana, Mississippi, Oklahoma, South Carolina, and Texas—actually have "no promo homo" laws that prohibit acknowledging the LGBTQ+ community or require that this community is portrayed in a negative light, if it is discussed at all.[12] Everyone deserves to feel safe in school. Teaching our children about the spectrum of sexualities and gender identities is a critical part of creating a safe learning environment for all. Imagine the isolation a child feels when sitting in a class that covers important topics and realizing that their gender identity or sexual orientation is left out of sex ed. While there are overlapping issues that are applicable to all humans, regardless of how one identifies, there are unique health and social considerations for individuals who identify as LGBTQ+ that must be part of the curriculum. Youth who identify with the LGBTQ+ community are at greater risk for HIV and STIs. Abstinence-only curricula do not include information to protect them from these risks.

Comprehensive sex education includes information about LGBTQ+ identities in a manner that is affirming and promotes health, safety, and respect for these teens. Teaching young people about the array of sexualities and gender identities is critical to promoting LGBTQ+ equality. Sex ed that leaves out these issues or portrays the LGBTQ+ community in only negative terms is not only isolating but also puts LGBTQ+ individuals at greater risk of self-harm and bullying. Inclusive education, on the other hand, can literally be lifesaving. It is validating and sends the message that every child matters regardless of what they identify as. We owe it to our kids to include the spectrum of sexual identities and expressions in their sex education for optimal health outcomes. Moving beyond a binary labeling structure of female/male and gay/straight will empower our youth to make the best decisions for themselves and live their best and healthiest lives.

Youth of Color

Truly comprehensive sexuality education programs address the communities they serve. This includes providing information in a manner that supports the linguistic and cultural needs of the student body without the racial prejudice and systemic racism that has historically portrayed people of color in inaccurate ways. Rates of teen pregnancy and STIs have perpetuated racial prejudices, as higher rates of these are found within Black and Hispanic communities. These statistics are typically shared without providing supporting information about the social determinants of health that unfavorably impact youth of color. Pulled out of context, such statistics are subject to misinterpretation and support a cycle of marginalizing communities who historically have been victims of prejudice and racism.

At a minimum, comprehensive sexuality education, like

other curricula, must be culturally competent so that it can be effective and reach its intended audience. Cultural competence takes into account the differences that exist within families regarding norms and beliefs that are part of students' identities. When this happens, sex education has a greater potential of reaching the diverse student body across all classrooms and affirming the sexual and reproductive rights of all people. So it's key to factor this kind of sensitivity into the learning environment to meet students where they are in a manner that is respectful to their culture while imparting medically accurate and developmentally appropriate information.

Youth with Intellectual and Developmental Disabilities

Children with intellectual or developmental disabilities (I/DD)—or having varying degrees of competency in reasoning, abstract thinking, and practical understanding—are more visible and accepted and more often part of mainstream schools than ever before. However, there remains a misconception that people with I/DD lack sexual desire due to what is misunderstood as immature emotional capacity. They are often perceived as eternal children. This, in fact, is incorrect. Sexual feelings, longings, and a desire for relationships are human nature and do not diminish according to intellectual capacity. The I/DD community, like all students, has the right to receive sex education that is delivered in a manner that is appropriate to their intellectual development.

Compounding this need is the difficult fact that people with intellectual and developmental disabilities are more likely to be sexually exploited. A body of literature indicates that sexual assault among people with I/DD occurs with greater frequency than with the general population. Children and teens with I/DD are three to four times more likely to be sexually assaulted.[13] Research suggests as many as 80 percent of women and 50 percent of men with I/DD will be sexually abused before the age of eighteen.

Withholding comprehensive sexuality education based on assumptions that someone does not need information or is too immature is negligent and discriminating. All students in school should have equal access to the sex ed that is offered, including a full discussion of consent and reporting. Students with I/DD have the same right to receive sex education as their peers, even if it is modified to match their learning abilities. If these students are not included in comprehensive sex education, they will remain more vulnerable to sexual exploitation.

Consent

This is another component of comprehensive sex education that is often overlooked or omitted from school curricula.

Teaching kids about their right to control who can touch their bodies begins at an early age. When my kids were younger, I would insist—against their wishes—that they honor Great-Aunt Betty's wish for a goodbye hug when she (practically a stranger to them) was leaving our home after a brief visit. Since then, I have realized that what I thought was a demonstration of warmth and good manners was a violation of my kids' boundaries. It does not matter why they did not want to hug Great-Aunt Betty. The fact that they were uncomfortable was reason enough. And yet my insistence perpetuated the message that their discomfort was less important than demonstrating good manners and not hurting Great-Aunt Betty's feelings. Instead, it would have been more appropriate for Great-Aunt Betty to ask their permission for a hug or for me to overtly give them the choice. Today, I have adapted my approach and no longer insist my kids hug anyone against their wishes.

As kids become older, the stakes become greater than merely enduring a hug from an unfamiliar relative with bad breath. Sexual consent is a person's right to make the choice about their sexual activity, every time. And to clarify, consent is not merely the absence of no. It is a two-way street that is active and ongoing between both partners. The absence of permission at any given moment by either individual is a violation of one's rights.

Teaching consent throughout childhood and the teenage years is critical to reinforcing that no means no, silence equals no, and everything other than explicit, unambiguous permission equals no, end of story. It does not matter if there was a yes in the past few seconds, weeks, or months. Everyone has the right to change their mind at any time. This is what consent is all about. Teaching the nuances of consent is important in the prevention of sexual assault. This means that age-appropriate consent topics are critical to a comprehensive sex-education curriculum.

What is the cost of not teaching the importance of consent? Sexual violence. We cannot adequately respond to this epidemic in America unless we raise children to fully understand concepts of consent, boundaries, and healthy relationships. Too often, consent discussions are not introduced until students are heading off to college, if at all. In reality, these talks need to start when children are much younger, and in ways that resonate with them as they grow emotionally.

PARENTAL CHALLENGE: Reviewing Your Experiences with Consent

Think about your own life experiences. Do you recall any incidents when you were subjected to participating in something against your will? What impact has it had on who you are today? How would you feel if your child had that same experience? How would it be different if they were the one who was being coercive?

Pleasure

One of the most common reasons why people engage in sex is for enjoyment. Do you recall learning this factual nugget during your sex education? I certainly did not. Sex for pleasure is not routinely acknowledged or celebrated in mainstream sex ed. Yet it accounts for the vast majority of sexual behavior—much more so than sex for the purpose of reproduction. Omitting the topic of pleasure from sexuality education is therefore shortsighted. It fails to teach people how to say yes to what they enjoy and no to what they do not. It also neglects a host of related topics, including the physical enjoyment of touch and connection and the importance of communication in sexual intimacy. The latter is a critical communication skill in sexual-violence-prevention efforts as well. Saying no to unwanted behaviors is easier when one feels empowered to say yes to what they do want.[14]

The public-health messages that promote risk-avoidance and risk-reduction behaviors need not be at odds with discussions about pleasure. Comprehensive sex education can and should be inclusive of discourse about sex for pleasure. Acknowledging the significant role that pleasure plays in sex is an important first step in advancing this discussion—it impacts all people regardless of sexual orientation and gender identity.

The pleasure discussion additionally removes the shame of exploring what feels good. It addresses the benefit of self-discovery and empowers people to listen to their inner voice about what they like and don't like, rather than the messages that are conveyed through scare tactics and peer pressure. Pleasure-based education empowers people to have healthy relationships with themselves and their partners. This sex-positive approach acknowledges that pleasure is a fundamental part of human experience.

This is yet another call to action to get involved in your child's sexucation. The next chapter offers insight on how you can start (or advance) your role as parent sex educator.

✳ 4 ✳

Get Involved in Your Child's
Sex Education

It is never too late to start or upgrade the level at which you talk with your kids about difficult subjects. Just because you have not had certain conversations before does not mean all is lost. In fact, there is no better time to start moving in this direction than right now.

Arm Yourself with Accurate Information

In Chapter 2, we talked about the different sources that may expose your kid to sex information. I hesitate to call those sources "sex education" if the information they present is not fact based and medically accurate or is created exclusively for entertainment purposes (e.g., porn). It should come as no surprise that your teen's use of social media contributes to their (mis)understanding and impressions of sex-related topics. It is one thing to comprehend the ease with which kids have access to online porn and feel sympathy for parents of those children. But it is another issue altogether to suspect or confirm that your own sweet pea is looking at it.

And they likely are. In the United States, 34 percent of youth between the ages of ten and seventeen intentionally viewed pornography.[15] This does not include people in this age group who accidentally stumble upon a porn site during a web search for something unrelated. Overall, approximately 73 percent of kids have viewed porn by age eighteen. There is also a common misconception that most viewers identify as male. Well, newsflash: 62 percent of girls and 93 percent of boys have viewed porn by this age.[16] These are likely underestimates given the increased access adolescents have to the internet today through smartphones and tablets.

Whether you feel your sex education was adequate when you were growing up is irrelevant at this moment. You and everyone else who reads this book now have the same opportunity to share useful, medically accurate, developmentally appropriate information with your kids regardless of what kind of sex education you received. Like with many subjects, the level of sex information that adults possess varies tremendously. Wherever you fall on the sex-education knowledge spectrum, you are perfectly positioned to be a primary provider of information for your kiddos. That is what libraries, books, and reliable internet sources are for. In addition, since our sex ed days, there have been significant updates in the terminology used and developments in our under-

standing of health issues. Also, there is now a broader recognition of sexual and gender identities, a forever-changing
landscape of access to services, and an astonishing array of
contraceptive methods to choose from. So even if you feel
you have a good grasp of things in this department, it's not a
bad idea to brush up on current sex-education content.

We Are in This Together

So many parents have expressed to me that they are uncomfortable talking with their kids about sex-related stuff. This
is a common sentiment, and it applies to topics that run the
gamut from bras and periods to consent and oral sex. Avoiding challenging conversations is not a unique phenomenon,
and I hope you find comfort knowing that you are not alone
in this. This is difficult stuff for so many people.

To assess your comfort level in this department, imagine that you are at the beach. Are you a splash avoider? A
wader? A deep diver? There is no right/wrong or good/
bad with these categories. Whichever one you relate to the
most makes perfect sense for you and is useful to identify
in order to elevate your self-awareness about such matters.
Self-awareness is the first step in moving in the direction
you want to go.

Many adults have found themselves on the sandy shores
of Lake HereWeGo. How they respond to the shimmering

water before them varies and falls into one of three distinct buckets. The descriptions of each bucket will help you determine which group you identify with the most.

Splash Avoiders

This group of parents stands far from the water's edge, avoiding getting wet or even slightly splashed. They take in the vastness of the lake before them and appreciate the view from the comfort of the warm sand. These parents find the act of getting into the water to be too much of an effort and rather uncomfortable. The initial shock of the cold water, the hassle of drying off, battling the stubborn sand that clings to their bodies, and managing wet hair afterward are not worth the benefits of going for a dip. By anchoring themselves away from the water, this group enjoys the scenery, sounds, and smells without actually going into the water.

How does this translate to talking with kids about sex? This equates to parents who are sex-talk evaders. They anticipate their kids will receive their sex education through means other than themselves. They might not know exactly where that is, but it certainly will not be from them, and they are perfectly okay with this.

Waders

This second group of parents enjoys the feel of the water on their feet and will walk to the water's edge, perhaps up to their knees. They appreciate the refreshing feel of the cool water and are comfortable staying in the shallow waters of Lake HereWeGo, knowing the benefits without feeling a strong desire to become fully immersed.

How does this translate to talking with kids about sex? Similar to lake waders, parents who wade into talks about sex are comfortable talking with their kids to some degree. They speak broadly about particular aspects of sex, are selective about what topics they broach, and respond to questions in brief but limited detail.

Deep Divers

This last group of parents enjoys Lake HereWeGo in its entirety. These are the folks who cannot get in the water quickly enough, diving in headfirst without hesitation. The irresistible lake is an invitation these parents cannot resist, and they enjoy the opportunity to swim, play, and experience the water for all it offers.

How does this translate to talking with kids about sex? Parents who fall into this classification are the most fearless group when it comes to initiating ongoing discussions of sexual health with their children. Nothing holds them back from offering information and answering questions while creating an environment that promotes openness.

DID YOU KNOW?

Time and time again, teens rank parents as the main influence in their sexual decisions. Capitalize on this relationship by getting comfortable talking openly with your children.

Get Out of Your Own Way

So why are you not involved in your child's sex education? While it's something you acknowledge you want to do, you might admit that you have avoided or minimized it for one reason or another. Or maybe you have tackled it and feel inadequate given how challenging it is. Let's face it: one of the biggest obstacles—if not THE biggest obstacle—to talking with our kids about sex is *ourselves*. Our own discomfort looms large, a prominent wall we are up against that feels overwhelming when we think about how to get around it. That is precisely why I wrote this book. We parents may have the best intentions of wanting to be open, easygoing, and able to talk with our kids about anything. Yet we sometimes fall flat when it comes to talking with our kids about sex and other tricky subjects. When we stop to observe it, our internal dialogue in this area is likely making every excuse to avoid these difficult conversations. Fears prevent us from moving because that internal dialogue gets in the way. And a common reaction to fear is avoidance. Therefore, we might be dodging important conversations with our kids because we are afraid.

PARENTAL CHALLENGE: Tapping into Your Feelings about Your Child's Sex Education

To help you chip away at the inner blocks that prevent you from talking with your child about sex, try this simple exercise to become more aware of those thoughts. It takes only a few minutes, and its questions are intended to help you get in touch with your feelings about initiating these critical conversations. Do this when you are in a comfortable environment and can give it your undivided attention. Write your responses in the space provided or in a separate document.

Why is it important for your child to receive accurate sex education?

Where do you want your child to learn about sex?

How important is it for you to be their primary resource in this area?

What prevents you from asking your child what they know about sex and how they learned it?

What fears do you have about talking with your child about sex?

What would make conversations with your child easier to initiate?

What concerns do you have if you do NOT talk to them?

What do you notice as you read your answers? In other words, what do you realize about yourself and your views on your child's sex education? It's possible that other parents who are struggling with sex conversations with their kids share some of the same concerns. Here are some of the responses I received from parents in the past. See which of these resonate with you.

Why is it important for your child to receive accurate sex education?

- "So she can make informed decisions and explore her sexuality in a responsible way."

- "To have a healthy attitude toward sex and to receive accurate information."

- "So she understands and can identify truth from false information."

- "To develop more confidence in an area that is somewhat less talked about openly."

- "So she is fully informed and can have a positive, healthy, and safe sex life when the time comes."

- "To support a well-informed decision-making process."

Where do you want your child to learn about sex?

- "Ideally from me and my partner at home, but it can also be supplemented by trusted members of our inner circle."

- "At home or in my community."

- "Home or in class at school."

- "From a trusted and knowledgeable source where she feels comfortable."

- "All areas: school, healthcare provider, and us (parents). Having information come from many sources helps the learner take in what they are able to in different settings."

- "We parents and other important people in her life, plus ongoing curriculum in middle and high school."

How important is it for you to be their primary resource in this area?

- "Very important."

- "Not that important where she learns the information as long as it is accurate and reliable."

- "The priority is that she receive accurate information from a primary source, and I am a secondary resource for advice and support."

- "It's important for the information to come from different 'experts' around them (caregivers, teachers, health professionals, LGBTQ+ community, etc.)."

What prevents you from asking your child what they know about sex and how they learned it?

- "It never seems like a good time."

- "It can be awkward and I'm unsure how to start."

- "My own discomfort; I was raised where we just didn't talk about sex and sexuality."

- "My teen's embarrassment/annoyance."

- "Lack of time in the day."

What fears do you have about talking with your child about sex?

- "Getting shut down."

- "Making my child feel uncomfortable."

- "Unsure what to say."

- "Afraid I'll be asked questions that make me uncomfortable."

- "It will feel awkward."

- "She won't pay attention."

- "My embarrassment."

- "Worried I'll be judgmental and she'll shut down."

- "Concerned I'll be insensitive and make assumptions."

What would make having conversations with your child easier to initiate?

- "Some guidance on when, what topics, and how to start conversations."

- "Making talks regular and brief so they are 'no big deal.'"

- "A parent group facilitated by a sex educator with model responses/language in tandem with comprehensive sex ed occurring at school."

- "Weaving sex talks into everyday conversation so it's not so difficult to discuss."

- "Parental prompts to follow up with what was taught in sex-ed class."

- "More time and my offering reassurance that I won't judge."

- "An age-appropriate bullet list to consult."

What concerns do you have if you do NOT talk to them?

- "She will get inaccurate information from other places (porn sites, peers, media, etc.)."

- "She will be confused and lack knowledge to feel good about herself."

- "She will engage in unsafe sex, develop low self-esteem, or won't advocate for her pleasure."

- "She will believe myths about sex and sexuality and not challenge repressive beliefs."

- "She will think of sex as something to be embarrassed about."

- "She will view sex as something to provide in order to please boys."

- "Sex will be all the more exciting to try if it is taboo."

- "She will not know that sex is positive."

- "She won't feel she has the ability to control her own body and pleasure."

Oftentimes, when we're trying to discover internal roadblocks that are getting in our way, we are not cognizant of our true thoughts and feelings until we hear ourselves say them aloud. We might have inner dialogue or "noise" that gets in the way of our ability to hear and comprehend what is at the root of our concern. Through self-examination, you can peel away, layer by layer, what is truly in the way. By getting in touch with this information, you can create important self-awareness, a key first step in moving forward.

Envision it this way: You are one of those Matryoshka dolls, those colorfully painted Russian dolls that decrease in size as they nest inside one another. Just as each wooden doll allows you to access the one that sits immediately inside it until you reach the innermost doll, probing questions allow you to get closer and ultimately access what is at the root of your own feelings. This is a useful visual that depicts the kind of uncovering that takes place through prompted self-discovery. To reach each "nesting doll" within you requires deep listening to reveal the true barrier at play. If this sounds confusing, read over this fictional dialogue between a parenting coach and a mother who wants to talk to her daughter about sex.

> **Coach:** "What brings you to coaching today?"
>
> **Dana:** "I have a tween daughter on the cusp of puberty, and I want to talk with her about the birds and the bees. But every time I try to start a conversation, I get all tongue-tied and end up chickening out."
>
> **Coach:** "It is scary for a lot of parents to talk about sex with their kids. Why are you at a loss for words when you attempt to start a discussion?"
>
> **Dana:** "I don't know. On the one hand, I know how important it is for her to get this information from me. On the other hand, it's as if my brain gets

in my way. I start to overthink, and it gets me nowhere but anxious. I just want her to have good, solid information that is accurate and reflects my values."

Coach: "It makes sense that you want what is best for your child with your personal values conveyed at the same time. Why is this important to you?"

Dana: "I did not have anyone who talked to me about this stuff when I was her age. As a result, I was confused, to say the least. There was a lot of stuff I believed that I eventually learned was flat-out incorrect. I don't even know where I got my misinformation. I think it was in dribs and drabs from various places—cafeteria talk, my friends with older siblings, TV . . . I'm too embarrassed to even say out loud some of the myths I carried until I was an older teenager."

Coach: "It sounds like you care about your daughter very much and do not want her to be uncomfortable like you were when you were her age. Why is this coming up now?"

Dana: "Hmmm, I am not sure. Well, she is twelve, and that is how old I was when I got my period, and I always felt embarrassed by it. No one prepared me for it, and the only talk I remember having at home about it was when my mom told me pads are under the bathroom sink when I told her I got my first period. Then one day, not long after that, my grandma scared me into believing I could get pregnant at any moment. I kept thinking I'd wake up one day with a spontaneously enlarged pregnant abdomen. I was seriously frightened this would happen. I don't want my daughter to go through adolescence with this kind of fear. The kind that comes from lack of factual info."

Coach: "That sounds terrifying."

Dana: "It was. It didn't help that when I asked my mom anything even remotely related to sex, I was met with 'Why are you asking? You don't need to know this stuff. You are too young.' And that was the end of that."

Coach: "It sounds like you grew up in a home where discussions of sexual health were discouraged. No wonder this is hard. I commend you for wanting your daughter to have a different experience than you did. You sound like you are very invested in your daughter's health and happiness. How fortunate she is to have you rooting for her."

In the example here, Dana shares her wishes that her daughter be spared the embarrassment and discomfort she experienced at a similar age. She recognizes she can play a positive role in making this happen. Like many parents, what she wants to do and what she feels she can do are not initially in sync. This is normal. We often feel we cannot do something for reasons that may not be easy to articulate or pinpoint. In Dana's case, her discomfort is not unusual for someone who grew up in a household where she received the message that talking about anything sex-related was not okay. This carried over into Dana's adulthood in the struggle she experienced when confronted with talking to her own daughter. Her desire to give her daughter the very thing she had wished for at a similar age was at odds with her comfort level because of the only family model she knew. Dana wanted to break the cycle by offering her daughter a safe and comfortable environment to talk about what she herself could not when she was the same age. This concept of working through the thoughts and other obstacles that prevent us from having conversations we want to have is explored further in Chapter 8.

Be a Safe Person Who Openly Offers Information

Since I am very comfortable talking about sex, it makes sense that I would have frequent but brief age-appropriate discussions with my two kids. These mini-talks have been ongoing, and when I ask them now, as older teens, what they remember about the talks we had during their upbringing, they joke that they had more chats on the subject than they care to remember. In our house, it was not uncommon for me to raise a topic around the dinner table. Though it was sometimes met with groans and eye rolls to denote "not again," it helped normalize what often feels awkward or off-limits among some families.

When my oldest was about ten years old, I came to the conclusion that it would be beneficial if my husband got in on the game. I felt that if our boys heard a thing or two about sex from their other parent, they would see this wasn't exclusively my territory and that their father was knowledgeable in this area to some degree. With a little persuasion and a lot of encouragement from me, my husband rolled up his sleeves and went for it.

He went into our son's room, ready to have a heart-to-heart talk about the metamorphosis that our son's body would soon undergo and new feelings he would experience due to increased hormones. Feeling pretty good about having shared such intimate information with our son, my husband concluded the discussion with the question "Is there anything you want to ask me?" After a lengthy pause and with a wrinkled brow, our son replied, "Yes! Who do you think is a better pitcher, Tim Lincecum or Jon Lester?"

This is one of my favorite stories in our household. It is

77

a wonderful reminder that we parents can get worked up about having conversations with our kids that are not always as big of a deal as we think. It is natural that we worry about broaching certain subjects with our kids, but what purpose does that worrying serve?

DID YOU KNOW?

It's never too soon to start talking with your kids. Sex education can begin when children are toddlers, at a developmentally appropriate level that matches your child's age/maturity. For a very young child, a good place to begin is teaching them the correct names for all of their body parts, including their genitals. A natural place for this to occur is during bath time or while getting them dressed. Using proper terms (e.g., *penis* rather than *wee wee*; *vulva* rather than *vagina*) is important and allows children to accurately communicate any health issues if they ever get sick or injured in their private parts.

Over the next few chapters, we'll cover four steps that will help you get on track for playing a more proactive role in your child's sexucation, regardless of what you have done in that respect thus far. And believe it or not, you might find it enjoyable. It is certainly better than doing it alone with self-doubt and a lack of confidence. These steps are simple and concrete and will help evaporate your concerns of figuring it out on your own with the requisite sweats and stomach knots. They're best followed in the order in which they're presented, but trust yourself if you feel the desire to rearrange them. The most important thing to remember—to borrow from a famous athletic company's logo—is to just do it, period. Going through these steps will alleviate stress and anxiety by creating awareness about yourself, your child's formal education at school, and your local community. In so doing, it will help boost your confidence so dreaded talks become a thing of the past.

And the first of those steps? Getting in touch with your own values about sex.

Part Two

THE FOUR-STEP PROCESS TO TALKING WITH YOUR KIDS ABOUT SEX

✳ 5 ✳

Step 1—Get in Touch with
Your Values about Sex

S o how do you move from the overwhelming feeling of "Yikes, where do I begin?!" to a place where you can stop, catch your breath, and realize you've got this? In this first of the four steps, let's understand what it means to live by your values and, more specifically, examine your sexual values. It might surprise you to learn that you have sexual values, especially if you have not thought in these terms before. But let me assure you that you do have them.

First, let's start from a common understanding of what life values are before we delve into sexual values. Values, per the definition I've developed over time, are our firmly held beliefs, the ingrained principles that are important to us and that we strive to live by. Consciously or subconsciously, values describe who we are and what we hold near and dear to us. They also drive many of our behaviors as long as they are not in conflict with something else. For example, I love the outdoors and make sure I get outside to enjoy nature on a regular basis. However, if there is a rainstorm, my value to stay comfortable (warm and dry) at that moment supersedes my desire to go for a walk or hike. In this way, I honor the outdoors from the comfort of my home by appreciating the view and the sounds of the storm from inside.

Values come from a variety of sources, one being the environment in which we were raised. Our family, peers, culture, religion, politics, media, and teachers initially shape our values. As we evolve and grow into our selves, we either adopt or adapt the values that have surrounded us throughout our lives. In some cases, our values will resemble those of our close family members or any group with whom we identify. Alternatively, we might find that our values veer away from those of our parents or other key influencers for a variety of reasons, such as not identifying as much with these individuals as we grow older. Our pasts play a role in shaping our value system, one way or another.

Values can be classified into two groups: fear-based or conscious-based. Fear-based values are those we have adopted to avoid something undesirable. They follow an "I need to do this or else . . ." format. An example of a fear-based value is "timeliness." I am one of those people who hates to be late. Arriving to an event by the designated time does not fill me with joy or gratitude. Being on time for me is about avoiding the stress of rushing or being late and possibly missing something important. If I were to look back on my life, I would not be surprised if there was a time when, as a sensitive adolescent, I was either privately reprimanded or publicly embarrassed for being late. If my need to be on time was problematic, I would seek therapy. However, it has not been a source of dysfunction to my knowledge—this is merely an observation about myself. Whatever the history of my compulsion to be on time, I have incorporated it into something I value.

In contrast to fear-based values are conscious-based values, which are aligned with what we want and what motivates us through deliberate steps to live intentionally. One example of a conscious-based value that is important to me is connection. The personal connections I forge with people mean the world to me. These connections fill my soul, energize me, and give me joy. If I am feeling blah, checking in with a loved one or interacting with someone from my professional circle by phone or in person will lift my spirits. Interpersonal connections have a way of boosting me and putting me back on track with whatever I have set my mind on doing.

When we live by our values, we live authentically and experience greater happiness, more fulfillment, and less stress. Do you know what you value most in life? It may be family, education, social connection, money, saving the planet, or something else. There are no right or wrong answers. It is simply a matter of knowing what matters most to you and then honoring those values and, thus, yourself. I examined my own values while becoming a certified life coach and I found it challenging to reduce a long list of things I held dearly and rank them in order of importance. Through that process, I realized that although my core values shift little over time, their ranking dances around according to circumstances in my life at any moment.

Take some time to get in touch with those things that matter most to you and think about how you are honoring them in your daily life. Understanding your deepest-held values and how they show up for you may take no time at all, or it may take several weeks of looking inward with the help of a coach. To reinforce the concept of values and how they express themselves in our lives, here are a few questions with my responses to illustrate how values show up.

Q: Think of a time when life was good. What value was being honored or expressed?

A: For me, it was when I traveled with my hubby and two teens to a tiny remote island where we stayed in a thatched-roof hut. There was no Wi-Fi, limited electricity, beautiful sunrises and sunsets, hammocks, swimming, snorkeling, and plenty of siesta time. The three days we spent there were incredible. We read, played card games, enjoyed the environs, and had wonderful conversations—life felt simple and grand. My values of family and connection were honored in such a reverent manner that I keep wondering if/how I can recreate a similar scenario.

Q: Think of a time when you were upset. What value was being challenged?

A: Not long ago, we lost our family dog. Opal died unexpectedly from a heart tumor that developed practically overnight. The loss of a beloved pet can feel devastating; her demise sent me into a downright depression that eased a bit with each passing week. She was an integral part of our family, and without her, three values I hold dearly were tested: productivity, connection, and nature. In addition to the grief that accompanies the loss of a furry family member, I realized much of my relationship with her tapped into key parts of who I am and how I live:

- She contributed to my feeling *productive*. Taking care of her with regular exercise and proper nourishment and keeping her healthy with routine checkups and prophylactic meds contributed to my feeling of purpose while she made me laugh and was a reliable source of joy each day.

- The *connection* I felt with her, including my ability to

read her body language and communicate with her, was as strong as those connections I feel with some of my closest human friends.

- Opal got me outside for my *nature* fix on a daily basis. Sure, I can and do go without her, but doing it with her felt much more enjoyable. She motivated me to get out and move. Plus, seeing her enjoy the smells and textures of the trails we frequented boosted my happiness.

Q: When do you compromise your values? Why?

A: I put a premium on self-care, and I encourage clients, friends, and family members to build self-care practices into their lives. And yet, when I am feeling stretched for time, my own self-care is one of the values that gets compromised. When I have a limited amount of time, my immediate reaction is to let self-care fall to the bottom of the list and prioritize my work and family needs. Ironically, this is precisely the time I need it the most. I pause and catch my breath to see where I might squeeze in some "me" time. Sometimes I can make it work. And yet other times, I allow deadlines and familial responsibilities to take precedence over a self-care activity. When this happens, the secondary challenge is to not allow resentment to creep in and recognize that it was *my choice* to postpone self-care.

Here's an example of how my personal values have impacted my family. One time, a mother from my local community who I've always admired for her well-organized household, common sense, and humorous attitude asked if my then twelve-year-old son could join a small group of boys she was going to take to dinner to celebrate her son's thirteenth birthday. "Sure," I replied. "Where are you going?"

"We are going to Hooters," she said. "They have really good wings."

I burst into laughter until I registered the expression on her face. She wasn't joking. I froze. Hooters conflicts with my value system by using women's physical features—notably their breasts—to appeal to their customer base as a marketing ploy. Their waitresses are used as objects, their bodies on display while they take your order and display great hospitality. Permitting my adolescent son to attend another boy's birthday party there conflicted with how I was raising him. "No, he can't go," I replied in a less than gracious voice, since I had been caught off guard.

While I am personally put off by the Hooters concept, it does not offend everyone, and that is okay. Values vary person to person, and it is these differences that we want to embrace. I was not comfortable allowing my twelve-year-old to patronize a restaurant where the servers are required to flaunt their "goods" (and I don't mean food). The restaurant conflicted with my goal of teaching my kid the importance of respecting women without objectifying them. Allowing him to go did not support a value I modeled. And of course, not everyone holds this same value, otherwise businesses like Hooters would not survive. I hoped the other mother respected my value-based decision, and I respected that we had differing opinions on the matter.

Afterward, I used the Hooters invitation as an opportunity to have a candid discussion with my son about why he wouldn't be joining the small gathering of friends. This was a wonderful teachable moment—even if he was disappointed that he missed the birthday celebration, it was a temporary letdown in exchange for a lifelong value I was hoping to impart.

Sexual Values

Now that we have passed Life Values 101, we can examine our sexual values. Just as we hold certain fear-based or conscious-based life values close to us, we have a value system in regard to sex. The next Parental Challenge is eye-opening for the simple reason that it requires you to pause and reflect on your values about sex and sexuality. This may be the first time you have been invited to answer a series of questions about your sexual values, so these questions can help you identify and articulate what you might not have ever put into words before. We carry all of the answers inside us, but we sometimes don't see them until we are prompted to make a deliberate effort to identify them.

As you read the questions, jot down your initial responses. Overprocessing can sometimes lead us to think about how we *should* answer, as opposed to identifying our personal truth. Remember, there is no right or wrong. This is simply an opportunity to be honest with yourself.

PARENTAL CHALLENGE: Identifying and Understanding Your Sexual Values

PART I

At what age do you feel it is appropriate for kids to start to learn about sex?

From whom do you feel they should learn about it?

How do you define sex?

What are your feelings about sex outside of marriage?

Same-sex intimate relationships are normal and healthy.
(True/False)

Your child comes out to you as gay. What is your response?

Your child comes out to you as transgender. What is your response?

How important is it that teens know about various birth control methods and safe sex practices?

When do you think kids should learn about birth control and safe sex?

How important is it *to you* that two people are in love before they engage in sexual behaviors?

How do you define consent?

What role does consent play in an intimate relationship?

To what extent do your values influence those of your kids?

It is natural for young people to masturbate. (True/False)

Where do your values about sex and sexuality come from?

PART II
After you have completed Part I, go back and read your responses aloud. Which answers stand out most for you?

How surprised are you about any of your responses?

To what degree do your responses coincide with your overall value system?

To what extent do they differ?

What questions, if any, left you feeling conflicted, even if only a small amount?

Next, let's examine how you are doing in communicating your sexual values with your children. It is possible that you are talking with your kids about values more than you realize. Perhaps you find it easier to talk about your sexual values but more difficult to talk about puberty, STIs, birth control, unintended pregnancy, porn, etc. Again, there is no right or wrong here. What is important is that you are open to exploring where you are in these areas. And depending on where you are, there likely is at least a bit of room, if not a giant gateway, to improve the channels of communication with your child so these conversations happen. Do not expect to observe an overnight change in your communication guts. This is a process, a spectrum that you will inch along, maybe slowly at first, but then at increasing speed as your confidence builds. You are already on your way, whether you realize it or not.

Our values come out in ways we don't always realize. "Johnny, clean up your room" tells your kid that you value a tidy house. How you spend your money (priorities), talk back to the news on the radio (political triggers), and respond to drivers who cut you off (injustice) are other examples of how our values leak out of us without making a formal declaration about such matters. Without always realizing it, we are conveying our values to our children all the time. And they are observing, even when we do not think they are paying attention.

In that same vein, think about what sexual values you are expressing to your kids. What comments or body language do you share, overtly or discreetly, in reaction to something you see or hear? Remember, your kids are always observing and taking cues from you. Sometimes we parents think we are fabulous actors who can disguise our reactions and keep our feelings from our kids. But most children are tuned-in, picking up on our subtle cues and assessing our opinions and values, whether we realize it or not.

Also, think about what conversations you can start with your child that reflect your values regarding sex. Keep in mind that this is an ongoing, lifelong process. This helps ease the pressure of thinking you have only one shot at this. These talks should also be frequent so that you can capitalize on organic opportunities that present themselves, such as when the same-sex couple across the street announces they're pregnant and your nine-year-old is left wondering how that's possible, or when you are driving with your teen and the radio news headline is an update about the nationally publicized college sexual assault case where the survivor was passed out from alcohol during her assault. So be intentional about these conversations. Should you choose to capitalize on such opportunities to talk with your child (nudge nudge), what personal values do you want to convey? How difficult does this feel?

The purpose of getting in touch with our values is to

help us become aware of them and how they show up in our daily lives. By creating space in our busy schedules—such as taking intentional moments of reflection, as we did through the Parental Challenge earlier in this chapter—we allow our core values to surface. Awareness of these values is key to incorporating them comfortably as we talk with our children about sex and beyond.

* 6 *

Step 2—Determine Which Sex-Ed Topics Are Taught in School

During one of our earliest Girls' Group meetings, I announced, "Let's do a quick review of the changes that occur at puberty. And then we can move on to some other material that might be new to you." In my mind, we would not need to spend a great deal of time on the nuts and bolts of pubescent changes, since these thirteen-year-old girls would definitely have learned them by now between school and home—or so I had assumed.

As I led the group in a multiple-choice trivia game on the topic, though, it quickly became apparent that I would need to modify what I had planned for the day. I had assumed that the girls were more or less in the same place with respect to their baseline knowledge of anatomy and the corresponding vocabulary for terms associated with puberty. Interestingly, their levels of awareness varied considerably, and my use of proper, scientific vocabulary only created further confusion, as it did not always match the lingo they used. So when the word "erection" came up, I was met with the girls' awkward silence.

Was this embarrassment? After a longer-than-expected period of quiet, one of the girls finally asked, "Do you mean 'boner,' Andrea?" It was then that I truly grasped how the use of words is yet another example of where we make assumptions. Not only did the girls vary in their level of knowledge, but we did not always speak the same language for some of the material we discussed. This was a tremendous eye-opener for me.

What did I take away from this *erection* vs. *boner* discussion? First, it reminded me that I cannot make any assumptions about the knowledge an individual may possess on a given topic. Just because someone is a certain age, has a particular physical appearance, gives off an air of knowing confidence, or displays great intelligence in other subjects, it does not necessarily translate into having a broad knowledge of puberty, or any subject for that matter. Second, although the girls had technically gone through the same formal sex-ed lessons at school (which were paltry at best), their level of recall varied, and there were no subsequent lessons to reinforce and expand upon their prior learning.

Up until this point, the public-school education in our district consisted of two lessons during fifth-grade gym class, led by the physical education teacher, devoted to discussing body changes at puberty. That was almost two years prior to the erection vs. boner discussion around my dining room table, seemingly a lifetime ago in the lives of these middle schoolers. And there had been no additional lessons since that time. Imagine what's going on with kids at this age developmentally, with no curriculum at school to help them make heads or tails of the physical and emotional changes they are experiencing.

What this particular Girls' Group gathering left with me was the realization about just how much many of us hope that schools will teach our children about sex—in this case, the developmentally appropriate topic of puberty. And by teach, I do not mean preach. My definition of teaching is to impart knowledge with factual support in a manner that is developmentally appropriate to the intended audience. Rather than a litany of facts, rules, or strict edicts, these lessons should be informative, unbiased, and descriptive, using appropriate language that kids can comprehend and delivered in a way that welcomes questions.

PARENTAL CHALLENGE: Naming That Word

This is one of my favorite educational games from the Girls' Group meetings, adapted to be used with your family. It helps bridge the gap between you (or the group facilitator) and the participants (either your kids and their friends, or a group of teens similar to the Girls' Group) and gets everyone on the same page. It is also a fun way to help everyone relax and laugh and to encourage them to speak and write words that are often considered impolite or taboo at school and home.

First, write a scientifically correct sex-education word or term on a piece of paper. Next, have the kids brainstorm all of the synonyms for that word, no matter how crass or raunchy. Then, focus all future discussions using the original clinical term.

What ARE They Learning at School?

In most public schools in the United States, there are subject areas that you can reliably expect to be taught: English, math, social studies, and sciences. Some would argue that these are important foundation subjects that are springboards for future success. Meanwhile, I have heard countless times from high school kids that they don't know why they were required to study X (chemistry, classic literature, etc.), as they never planned to pursue professions that rely on knowledge of these subjects. In other words, the perceived utility of some subjects hovers around slim to none.

Conversely, sex education is a subject that will impact almost every single person, as most humans are sexual beings in one way or another. However, the frequency with which sex education is part of the standard curriculum is significantly less than precalculus and the sciences, for example. Without federal requirements, states and local school districts are left to their own devices to decide what is taught and when.

As mentioned throughout this book, sexuality education goes well beyond discussions of physical and emotional changes that accompany the transition from child to young adult. It encompasses critical information that we, as human beings, have a right to know. Not teaching about the diverse topics that fall under comprehensive sexuality education is a disservice to humanity. And yet, despite that more students will become sexual beings (if they are not already), experience physical desire, and seek reproductive health services than will require the use of their eleventh-grade chemistry lessons in their daily lives, sex education is taught with significantly less consistency, comprehensiveness, and medical accuracy than other subjects.

Many parents have a love/hate relationship with sex ed being part of their child's school curriculum. In one camp are parents who do not want their kids taught about sex at school for any number of reasons. Some may feel their kids are not mature enough for sex education; they worry it will encourage sexual behaviors, or they feel it is inappropriate to teach at school. In the other camp are parents who feel a degree of relief knowing that sex education is taught in the classroom. And it is possible to find oneself in both camps. Overall, more parents want sex ed for their kids at school. According to the Sexuality Education and Information Council of the United States (SEICUS), there is great support for comprehensive sex education. While public support for sex ed is major, just over one-third of US high schools and 14 percent of middle schools provide comprehensive information as defined by the CDC.[17] This suggests a significant opportunity for growth in this area.

In contrast to comprehensive sex ed, an abstinence-based curriculum (or sexual risk avoidance education) teaches that sexual activity is only appropriate between heterosexual married couples and should not occur outside of that union to avoid unintended pregnancy and sexually transmitted infections. Withholding other sexual-health topics means students receiving this curriculum are not given the tools and know-how to promote healthy behaviors and ubiquitous visibility for all students.

Examples of Comprehensive Sex-Ed Topics		
Puberty	Sexual Anatomy	Abstinence
Dating & Relationships	Consent & Communication	Sexual Decision-Making
Dating Violence	Gender Identity	Sexual Orientation
STIs & Prevention	HIV/AIDS	Contraception
Pleasure	Pregnancy	Pregnancy Options
Bullying	Diversity	Sex in the Media

Requirements for sex ed are determined partially by the state where you live and the individual school district. Therefore, it makes sense that what is actually included from district to district will vary tremendously in both the breadth and quality. Regarding what states require, the Guttmacher Institute found that only twenty states and the District of Columbia require the provision of information about contraception. Additionally, nineteen states require that information includes messages that sexual activity only be within the context of (heterosexual) marriage, and only nine states and the District of Columbia require the importance of consent to be covered.[18] You can read the Guttmacher Institute's report to see how things look in your state, or reference the chart on page 216.

As a parent, it is your role to be aware of what constitutes sex education in your child's school and to understand the particulars of how it is taught. Many parents rely on schools *exclusively* to offer sex education, so they don't just lean on the school for support in this area. They also depend on schools to teach the topics they want their kids to learn, topics that they feel too awkward to address . . . until now, that is.

This is where you can make a difference. You can become more involved in your child's sex education, not only by customizing discussions to incorporate the values you want to impart to your children (thus reinforcing that you are a trusted, go-to resource that they can seek out when needed), but also by gaining an understanding of what comprises sex education in your child's school district. And you'll likely be surprised not only by what, if anything, is taught at school, but also by the degree to which a school communicates with parents regarding the contents of the curriculum they use.

To help you assess what is offered in your district, here's a set of questions to help you gain perspective on what sex ed looks like in your local school system. These questions will help you navigate the sex education that is taught at school and assess how comfortable you are with it.

- Is sex education taught in your child's school? If not, why?
- What is the name of the sex-ed curriculum that is used?
- What topics are included?
- In what grade(s) is it taught?
- Is it evidence-based/informed?*
- Who teaches the classes?
- Does the teacher/facilitator have professional development to address comprehensive, inclusive topics?
- How are parents included in the education?

If you are wondering how to find this information, you are in good company. It can feel daunting and perhaps uncomfortable to take the steps to gather this info, so I have broken them down for you as follows.

---

* Evidence-based programs and practices are models that have positive effects on outcomes based on rigorous scientific processes. Evidence-informed programs and practices are informed by prior research but not limited to them. A list of evidence-based and evidence-informed curricula is provided at the end of the book.

Step A: Review Your School District's Sex-Ed Curriculum

This will mean visiting your school district's website and seeing if the curriculum overview, by grade, is publicly available. Sex education will likely fall under a larger topic such as "health and wellness," so you might have to do some digging. Additionally, sex education might be included but disguised under a different name, such as the name of the formal curriculum that has been adopted, or general vague terms such as "healthy relationships." If you cannot find any reference to what may be sexuality education, it does not mean it is not included. This is simply a nudge to move on to deeper sleuthing (a.k.a. Step B).

Step B: Reach Out to School Officials

There are many people who will likely have the information you are seeking, and it might feel confusing to know where to begin. First, reach out to your local school board. The school board consists of locally elected public officials charged with governing a community's public schools, setting policies that affect your child and your school. Sometimes there is a separate school health-advisory committee that could be another option for assistance in collecting the information you are seeking. Either of these should have a grasp of what is taught and be able to give you information. Incidentally, private schools and public charter schools are not part of these administrative bodies. They will have their own governing bodies that make decisions about curricula, so reach out to head administrators to obtain this information.

Offering sex education in school is a great first step. And, it is by no means the last one. Even if your child's school offers a robust curriculum that covers more than you could ever imagine, talking with your kids about what they are learning is key. And remember, you do not need to have all of the answers. Our children want to know they have a trusted adult they can go to, and you likely want to be that adult. Discussions about life, values, money, sex, relationships, the news of the day, etc. reinforce that you are someone they can go to with their questions.

Other Sources of Information in Your Child's Sex Education

Friends, Peers, Older Siblings, and Cousins

One of my most vivid memories involves a close high school friend sharing with me a step-by-step description of an intimate encounter she had with her longtime crush. Given my lack of experience in this area up to that point, I clung to every detail and asked for clarification to remove any possibility of ambiguity. I was on a mission to get an unfiltered account of the stuff I wasn't learning anywhere else. And at age fourteen, what better way to get my info than from a trusted friend with whom I spent countless hours talking about our crushes. Actually, there are many good, reliable methods to obtain information, and yet having a dear friend with firsthand experience was a bonus for my curious ears. However, one may not always receive reliably accurate information from young teens and peers, so having other trustworthy sources of information is imperative.

A child's older siblings and teen relatives may serve as information sources when it comes to learning about sex. And like with other influencers, the question remains: How reliable are they? Some relatives may intentionally withhold information from their younger siblings and cousins as a way of "protecting" them in a misguided attempt to prevent them from engaging in certain behaviors. Some siblings will inadvertently share inaccuracies and unknowingly perpetuate wrong information. And still, there are those older sibs and cousins who serve as reliable and useful go-tos to bridge the educational gaps, be they small cracks or hefty chasms.

The Internet

In Chapter 2, we established that the internet, for better or worse, offers a plethora of material for curious minds, and sexual content is no exception. It is a gateway for everything and anything one wants to know. Access to pornography understandably concerns many of us parents, as we have already discussed. However, there are other, non-porn internet sites that can be tremendously educational and helpful.

For anyone who feels left out of formal sex education, the internet can be an option for receiving information that acknowledges and validates them. In addition, the confidentiality proffered by accessing information via the internet can be a lifeline for adolescents who might otherwise feel excluded or ostracized if they do not fit a heterosexual norm or other mainstream category commonly taught through formal sex education in school.

While the internet can be an incredible resource for the most up-to-date services, products, and virtual communities in an inclusive manner, the accuracy of the information provided is potentially less reliable. Some groups use the internet to perpetuate non-truths, spread discrimination, and push their narrow agendas, so one must be sensible and exercise caution when seeking information through this channel. This means understanding the sources of information that appear in search results and ensuring they are valid resources.

PARENTAL CHALLENGE: Zeroing in on Your Child's Sources of Information

What and where your child is learning informally may reveal more than you expect. Parents are often surprised when they realize the information influencers in their child's life. Answer the following questions to assess your level of awareness in this area:

How familiar are you with your child's information sources?

What can you do to assess the accuracy of their sources of information?

How likely are you to ask them about what they know and from where they learned it?

Having a grasp on both the formal and informal sources of sex information your child receives can be eye-opening. In addition to school and informal resources, both of which might be lacking in breadth, depth, and accuracy of factual information, there are other options to explore to help with your child's sexucation. The next chapter dives into possibilities to explore in and around your community.

∗ 7 ∗

Step 3—Consider Community Resources

he landscape of community sex-education resources is inconsistent and uneven, from utterly barren to resource rich, with every imaginable terrain in between. Just as there are food deserts (those areas with limited access to affordable and nutritious food), there are so-called "sex-education deserts," or geographic regions—be they towns, cities, or states—where sex education resources outside of school are few and far between. My attempt to locate community sex-education program options outside of the classroom in my own area left me unsettled. In my attempt to generate useful search tips to share with you, I dug deep, exhausted search terms, and looked outside of the box before I reached an epiphany: if I, a seasoned public health researcher, was struggling to find resources, what would happen when others with presumably less research experience embarked on a similar quest? My efforts revealed that finding relevant programs can be difficult.

My great conclusion, therefore, is that with rare exceptions, the majority of us in the United States live in a sexual-education desert. Most certainly there are exceptions to this, and if you live in a region with access to comprehensive, medically accurate, inclusive sexuality-education community programs, you are fortunate. The options, breadth, content, and even factual accuracy will invariably differ from community to community, so it's important to explore the details of what comprises such programs to ensure a positive and healthy fact-based learning experience.

This section is meant to help you go about finding resources to assist in the comprehensive sexucation of your teen. To borrow from another saying, I am teaching you *how* to fish, rather than offering you a fish to feed your hunger. Once you know what you are looking for and where to look, you will be on your way to learning what is available locally. As I said earlier, the degree of variability will be huge, depending on where you live and what specifically you are seeking. If you live in a sex-education desert, or in an area that offers limited sex education based on values that do not reflect yours, fear not. Online resources offer access to anyone with an internet connection and are just a few keystrokes away. This is where the internet can work in your favor.

Additionally, later in this book I'll share the group discussion model I devised and spell out steps for you to create your own community group as another option. Sound daunting? I assure you it is not. If I did it by the seat of my pants, you can do it with my tried-and-true pointers outlined in subsequent chapters. And even if you are fortunate enough to live in a sex-education oasis, you might still be curious to start your own group. But more on that later.

Right now, it's time to examine other opportunities that might be available to you and your child for sex education within the local community. Besides schools and parents, what other options exist to help our kids reach their potential in making informed decisions as they grow up and become more independent? Community groups are certainly a viable option, assuming they are more or less aligned with your values and what you want for your children.

Keep in mind that having a community resource is a wonderful start *and* might be what you are looking for. However, understanding the program content is an important component of this, as an appealing sex-ed community program might actually be preaching abstinence-only without other topics. Similarly, they may include values that are not aligned with what you want for your child. Because you are reading this book, you may be looking for something more than the scare tactics and misinformation that have been known to accompany abstinence-only programs.

Where to Look in Your Community

National organizations with local affiliates and community-based programs are good areas to start your search. Here I reference a few standouts that have a presence at multiple locations around the country. There are hundreds of medically accurate sex-education programs at the local level that I cannot begin to list without doing extensive research. That's where you come in. You can do your own search in your local area. What's provided here will help you get the ball rolling and encourage you to find what is offered and accessible to meet your needs.

Our Whole Lives

This might sound counterintuitive, but one of my go-to places to inquire about sex-ed programs is church. Yes, you read that correctly. Specifically, the local Unitarian Universalist Church and the United Church of Christ, if either is accessible to you. Our Whole Lives (OWL) is a comprehensive sex-education program that is a collaboration between these two churches. This curriculum offers lifespan sexuality education using a holistic approach, tailored by age group. The program is secular, meaning the teachings are not religiously affiliated and welcome people from all faiths. Additionally, it is value-based and recognizes that parents are their children's primary educators. OWL places an emphasis on abstinence while offering comprehensive information.

If you are interested in this kind of program for your child, check to see if these churches are nearby. Next, reach out to them and inquire if they offer OWL (not all churches of these denominations will), then determine if this is a viable option for your child or family. Only you can make this determination, and I encourage you to do so by educating yourself about OWL. For me, it stands out as one of the most comprehensive and inclusive curricula out there. I personally love the emphasis on parent involvement—parents don't feel they are simply outsourcing the responsibility without remaining involved in this amazing part of child rearing.

A question that often comes up is, "If I do not know what I am looking for, how will I find it?" In other words, how would someone find OWL if they do not know the name? Well, since I didn't know names of particular programs when I was doing my search, I used descriptive words in my online search terms. I also tried different variations of such terms as "Boston sex ed" (since I live in the Greater Boston area), "local sex education for teens," and the like. The results were mostly published articles about attitudes and other relevant aspects, not a plethora of programs in my local community, and certainly not the results that I was seeking regarding sex education. If this happens to you, try other related search terms instead.

Planned Parenthood Federation of America

Planned Parenthood Federation of America is an organization with local health centers around the country. They not only are direct service providers, but also place a heavy emphasis on education and have a plethora of resources available to assist in the sexucation of our youth. Among their offerings are community partnerships that focus on equipping parents and caregivers to be the primary sexuality educators of their kids. Planned Parenthood's website can help you locate your closest health center, and the site also offers a wealth of other online educational resources for parents, schools, and students.

State and Local Health Departments

State and local health departments help fund community-based organizations, often earmarked for specific programs, which might include sex-education services. One way to learn about sex-education classes that are available through your local community-based organization is to look at your state's department of public health. A search on their website for "sex education" or "sexual health" can lead to useful information about what is available in your state, including a list of organizations that receive state funding specifically to provide such services. Among them are community health centers that provide educational services as well as clinical and preventive services to communities with limited access to healthcare (a growing segment of the US population). Sometimes, this requires a bit of digging and creative sleuthing that will hopefully reward you with useful information. Similarly, a search of your town's local health department is another way to find organizations, agencies, and programs that you did not know existed.

Health Care Providers

Pediatricians and primary care providers are uniquely positioned to be a rich resource for sexual health information during annual health maintenance visits to the doctor. When you think about it, who else has an ongoing connection with your child and is a trusted person with the qualifications to convey medically accurate information to your maturing child? The one-on-one nature of these visits allows the primary care provider to customize the message based on the developmental stage of the patient. Also, the patient may be emboldened to ask relevant questions without the embarrassment of a group setting. Discussions between an adolescent and their health care provider afford an opportunity for personalized, frank conversations and appropriate health promotion.

The primary care provider as sex educator might seem like a no-brainer. But guess what? Sex-education conversations between doctors and patients are not reliably taking place. Not all medical providers are at ease talking about sexual health with their adolescent patients; perhaps they do not want to take the time to open the big can of worms that is sex education. In a study of adolescent health maintenance visits with physicians, there was no mention of sexuality issues in one-third of adolescent annual visits. When sexual health was discussed, less than forty seconds was devoted to the subject area.[19] This points to the need for allocating sufficient time during a health visit to address all adolescent needs. Furthermore, a 2016 report by the American Academy of Pediatrics provides guidance to doctors who serve adolescents. The report recommends that medical training programs include interpersonal skills around sexuality discussions, how to navigate tough conversations, and information and skills to provide LGBTQ+ friendly care.[20]

Meet Them Where They Are

One of the key components to reaching the intended audience is accessibility. In other words, how easy is it for your target population (teens) to obtain the goods (sexucation) they require to live their healthiest lives? If a comprehensive sex-education curriculum is not available in school, and OWL or other community-based programming is not located near you, what options do you have?

If you build it, they will come . . . or will they? To minimize the possibility of access barriers, I prefer the "meet them where they are" approach. This means finding out which community locales and gathering institutions could be potential partners in offering sexucation that benefits youth, teens, and parents. In other words, where do people in your locality go to participate in community activities? These venues are worth exploring for collaborative opportunities to host sex education programs or seminars, if they are not already offered.

Here are some natural gathering places within your community to check out in this regard:

- **Public Libraries:** More than simply places that lend books, libraries are often major players in building community and offer (or are open to offering) classes and meetings in a central location.

- **Community Centers:** These public locations, if you are fortunate enough to have one in your city, lend themselves to community gatherings for specific activities, social support, information-specific meetings, and even recreation.

- **Youth Activity Centers:** These offer supervised environments for youth to participate in organized physical activities, arts and crafts, and even homework completion. Examples include YMCAs and Boys and Girls Clubs of America, as well as many others.

Take a moment to think about community settings in your area. What others can you think of? It is possible that after you do some research, you will feel there are no reasonable community options that are near you or are accessible for one reason or another. Despite your best intentions to find something, anything, you may still be on a quest for a community option. If that's the case, then check out Part 3 of this book, where I offer details on how to create a Girls' Group, a micro version of a community forum to respond to this need.

But before that, the next chapter reveals the fourth and final key step in becoming more comfortable talking with your child about sex. It describes a valuable communication strategy that is especially useful in easing your way into sex talks. It also offers easy tips that you can immediately put into practice.

* 8 *

Step 4—Pause, Ponder, Proceed

One of the challenges that comes with parenting is controlling one's impulse to react when our kids say things that catch us off guard or are fraught with misinformation. This is the difference between reacting and responding. By "respond" I mean taking a moment to pause, catch my breath, and be intentional in what follows. The pause can range from a few seconds to even a day or two. For example, when my son said he was not returning to his summer job as a sleepaway-camp counselor so he could "hang out" at home instead, it took all of my strength to calmly say, "That sounds interesting. I'd like to hear more about that later." Meanwhile, my inner dialogue was screaming, *Are you nuts? Why wouldn't you return to your dream job that you've been talking about all winter?* I broached the subject with him several hours later, when I was more composed and ready to ask open-ended questions so I could understand what was truly underneath his decision. This chapter describes how to apply a similar approach to overcoming certain thoughts that get in the way of moving in a positive and desirable direction.

Pause

We often create goals for ourselves with good intentions and set out to achieve them. And then we find ourselves stuck, distracted, or unable to make the strides we want, for one reason or another. How frequently have you found yourself wondering why you do not take action on things you thought were important? What excuses do you hear yourself saying aloud or in your head?

Examining the perceived barriers that get in the way of tangible steps toward our goals begins with a purposeful pause. My definition of "pause" in this context is an intentional break from the thoughts, self-talk, and beliefs that keep us spinning our wheels without any movement. Pausing is a step toward awareness. It makes it easier for us to see the landscape, hear the noise, and observe what is going on. How easy is it to see a painted mural on the side of the road when you are driving by at forty miles per hour? In contrast, what happens when you stop the car to examine the mural while staying still? The latter offers an opportunity to observe, to see, to feel.

Pausing is the first element in what I call the Pause, Ponder, and Proceed strategy. Doing this when we face obstacles allows space for us to challenge them. It enables us to identify *perceived* hurdles with more clarity. Once we learn how to pause, it becomes easier for us to ponder (which allows us to reflect and get in touch with what is behind the hurdles) and then proceed (which challenges our conceptions of what stands in the way and allows us to dismantle or maneuver around the hurdles). Sometimes this is easy. Other times, we have to slog through to achieve rewarding results. The outcome is the liberating feeling that results from having clarity and direction rather than the weight of roadblocks and uncertainty.

Ponder

There are reasons or excuses that we have for not doing things that we plan or want to do. With some examination, we can often cite what it is that prevents us from taking an intended action. These obstacles or barriers are either external or internal in nature.

External barriers are hurdles that are actual physical limitations to achieving a goal. These obstacles are constructs that are out of your control and prevent you from going where you want to go. Some external barriers may feel harder to overcome than others. For example, they might depend on factors such as a city bus schedule that does not align with your work hours, or the availability of a service provider you want to enlist. However, external barriers are typically easier to maneuver around than internal barriers, although the former may require some creativity and flexibility.

For example, Max has a comfortable relationship with his parents. When he hears that his best friend, Drew, is signed up for an eight-week life issues class on Saturday afternoons at the local Boys & Girls Club, he is curious and wants to participate. So he asks his parents if he can join Drew and sign up for the class. His parents remind him that they spend most Saturday afternoons with Grandpa, who lives in an assisted-living facility in a neighboring town. After some discussion, Max's parents suggest that they shift their visits with Grandpa to Saturday mornings or Sunday afternoons so that Max can attend the Saturday-afternoon class—an idea that Max agrees with wholeheartedly. In this example, time served as an external barrier. However, Max's parents recognized that they had options and could get around what stood in their way without too much effort.

Conversely, *internal barriers* are beliefs that serve as an undercurrent to our thoughts that get in the way of our taking action about something. They can show up as negative self-talk or limiting beliefs that prevent us from moving in a direction we desire. Internal barriers can show up as that nagging voice in one's head that conveys "I am not good enough" and are demotivating. Fear can sometimes be the underlying force behind internal barriers. Similarly, assumptions we make and conflicts with our values can get tangled in our self-talk and stop us in our tracks.

Let's say Cindy has noticed that her fifteen-year-old daughter, Anna, has been retreating to her bedroom more often. When Cindy passes by Anna's closed door, sometimes she hears Anna in a hushed phone conversation, but she does not intrude out of respect for her daughter's privacy. Then one Saturday morning, Anna comes into the kitchen for a late breakfast, and Cindy notices what looks like a hickey on the side of Anna's neck, obscured by her long hair. It catches Cindy off guard, and she chooses not to say anything, though her mind is racing with questions such as, *Where did this come from? Was this consensual? Were substances involved?*

As these thoughts swirl in her mind, Cindy wants desperately to talk with Anna about crushes, feelings, and sex. But she is frozen and does not know how to even start. Though her mind is active, her mouth has stopped working. Cindy is afraid of speaking up. Her fear of saying the wrong thing or exploiting Anna's privacy prevents her from being the source of information she would like to be for her daughter. In this case, fear is the internal barrier that is stopping Cindy from talking to Anna.

To complicate matters, internal barriers can sometimes present themselves as external barriers. We humans have an amazing ability to attribute our internal hang-ups to external causes. It can seem so easy to point our finger at something or someone else when we do not achieve a desired outcome. This is also true when it comes to understanding the internal and external barriers we confront.

For instance, does time seem like an internal or external barrier? With all of the juggling that comes with our work, family responsibilities, carpooling and commuting, extracurricular activities, etc., we find ourselves racing from one place to another, often exhausted, overwhelmed, and feeling like we need to catch our breath. But time is one of those constructs that is filled by things we prioritize. What do you do when your dear friend from Hong Kong whom you haven't seen in three years calls to say she'll be in town for a couple of days for a business trip and wants to get together? You make time for her. How about when the elderly widow who lives next door is recuperating from minor surgery and a December snowstorm dumps half a foot of snow in the middle of the night? You shovel her walkway before heading to the office. Did you factor that into your schedule? No. But do you make time for it nonetheless? Yes.

More than likely, when we declare we don't have time to do X, what we are really saying is, "We will not do X because of Y." The bigger question is, What is the Y? Is it fear disguised as busyness? Is it that deep down we do not truly want to do X, so we create barriers? It is common for internal barriers to masquerade as external barriers.

Proceed

One of the barriers that stops many parents in their tracks is their desire to have the perfect response, speech, or comments before talking with their children. When they do not feel confident about a topic, they tend to use that as an excuse to avoid the conversation altogether. Well, here's a news flash: no parent has all the facts when it comes to sex education. If we wait for that perfect moment, we will be waiting for a very long time. Remember, some information is better than none.

More important than breadth of information is accuracy. Sharing factual, medically accurate information is key, and even if you know very little (or nothing) about a particular topic, being open and willing to start a conversation is a great beginning. I find it empowering to admit when I do not know something. When I have conversations with my kids and they ask me something I do not know, I often say, "That is an excellent question, and I actually do not know the answer. Why don't we look it up and see what we learn?" This approach is useful for several reasons:

- It humanizes us by modeling that it is okay to not know all the answers, and it provides a beautiful opportunity to show we are comfortable admitting it.

- It demonstrates that we are interested in learning more and reinforces that learning is a lifelong process.

- It encourages side-by-side learning.

In short, focus on progress—not perfection—one baby step at a time.

Don't Know Where to Begin? No Problem

It is common to have much to say and not know how to begin. It may be equally unsettling to try to resume a conversation you previously started with your teen. At the other end of the spectrum is knowing when to stop. Much to the dismay of my kiddos, I still have a lot of work to do in reeling in my talks. I tend to be overly enthusiastic and thorough, so I miss social cues that my sons have had enough and it's time to let the topic rest. All of these scenarios are real challenges that you might face in knowing when and how to start the conversation. In fact, talking with your kids about sex is likely the number one subject that causes you to tense up and feel at a loss for words. You are part of a club that you never intentionally joined, with millions of other members who face the same struggles.

The good news is that you can drop your membership to this club at any time. No matter what is getting in the way of opening your channels of communication, it is temporary and surmountable. You don't have to be a creative genius or be amazingly articulate for this to happen. Perfectly imperfect is how I like to think of myself in regards to my parenting skills and communication with my kids. And it is the imperfection and honesty of being our authentic selves that makes us interesting and human.

Eight Tips for Having Successful Conversations with Your Child

Believe it or not, you have everything you need to tackle this. These eight tips are all accessible to you now, and some may already be part of your communication style with your child. As you read through them, note which ones you do routinely and which you want to work on. You have ample opportunity to practice these.

- **Keep it brief.** The reality is that many tweens and teens have shorter attention spans and lose interest when too much information is shared at once, especially when parents are the messengers. I often think my kids hear my words as "wa wa wa wa wa wa wa," just as the *Peanuts* characters hear the adults in their lives. Many of these talks will be impromptu, sparked by a news item on the radio when you are driving together, or an event at school your child shares with you.

- **Validate their questions.** Using a normal tone, acknowledge that what they are asking is a good question. This reassures them that you are open to their questions.

- **Admit what you do not know.** There will be questions for which you legitimately do not have an answer. Saying, "I'm not sure, so let's look this up together" is perfectly acceptable and makes you even more accessible by sharing your honesty.

- **Up the frequency.** Having many brief conversations rather than a single "talk" (which was more common when we were teens) is the way to go. Not only does this allow more opportunities to become comfortable with the subject of sex, but it also allows you the freedom to introduce topics as they arise, rather than having to have a cram session and risk leaving out important pieces. More frequent discussions also normalize sex talks so they are less awkward and taboo.

- **Verify they heard correctly.** Asking them if your answer makes sense is a way to make sure you answered what they asked in a way that is comprehensible.

- **Use the environment as a conversation prompt.** Opportunities to open a conversation are everywhere as long as you keep your eyes and ears open. Television commercials for sanitary products or erectile dysfunction pills are examples of good starting points. I recently asked my son if he knew the purpose of the product being touted when a commercial for Kyleena came on during a television show we were watching. Incidentally, it is a brand of intrauterine device (IUD), a long-acting, reversible birth control method that is placed inside a woman's uterus. Once you open your eyes and ears, you will notice that there are ample opportunities to (courageously) address a variety of important subjects that are not being broached elsewhere.

- **Find settings free of distraction.** One of my favorite places to have these conversations is in the car. With both my son and me facing forward (which makes it easier for the embarrassed teen to avoid eye contact) and nowhere to escape, it's a golden opportunity. Another favorite time was when I would say goodnight to my kids back when they went to bed before I did. They would often ask for a back scratch, and I would agree with one caveat: that the both of us would talk. This was a unique time when the boys would be more open. It was also a perfect setup, since they were lying on their stomachs (so they wouldn't have to make eye contact) and motivated to keep the conversation going to prolong the relaxing back scratch.

- **Timing is key.** You've heard that a poorly timed joke can fall flat, right? Well, timing is also a factor in a successful discussion. If you, your child, or both of you are tired, cranky, or in my case, *hangry* (short-tempered and unable to focus due to hunger), it is not an ideal time to have any important conversation, even if an external prompt has created a wonderfully teachable moment. In such a case, make a mental note of what you want to say and approach the subject when the timing is better, even if it is days away. This may sound something like, "Remember when we were driving home from soccer practice and we heard that story on the radio about . . ."

Write a Letter to Your Teen (or Tween)

Conversations are wonderful and encouraged, but they are not the only form of communication that can be effective. Sometimes, for any number of reasons, parents find it useful to rely on the written word. My preference is for spoken conversations. However, you know your child best, and if you feel like starting a conversation via notes, texts, or emails, go for it. The most important thing is that communication is happening.

I discovered my son had been viewing porn on
e when he was a middle schooler, I could not sit
l also recognized that he lacked the maturity to
have a face-to-face conversation about it with me. And to
be perfectly honest, I was grappling with my own immediate feelings after this discovery, so I implemented a version
of Pause, Ponder, and Proceed. The result was this message
that I wrote in a letter and left on his bed for him to read in
privacy and on his timeline. This is an example of knowing
your child best and adapting modes of communication that
are most suitable.

I will share a redacted version of the letter below. If you
find yourself in a similar situation with your child, feel free
to use this as a basis for your own written message.

Dear _____,

Let me start by emphatically stating I LOVE
YOU. You are an amazing person, and I am not just
saying this because you are my child. You are caring,
compassionate, funny, smart, multi-talented, and
fun to be around. Nothing will ever change how I
feel about you. And that's a promise.

I am writing you because I do not want you to
feel embarrassed or ashamed. I know that when I
talk with you directly about certain things, sometimes your embarrassment can cause you to get

mad at me or be less truthful, which is not uncommon for many people your age and even many older people. But that would not be good for either of us. Please understand this letter comes from a loving place in my heart, because I care about you and your well-being. This is not an admonishment.

It is totally normal to be curious about sex and want to see it, especially at your age and where you are in your development. This is a natural part of growing up. Unfortunately, internet porn shows sex in ways that are not often real. Actors and models are doing things for the entertainment of their audience, but those things are not very realistic. Think of a movie where there is a high-speed car chase that results in a dramatic crash with explosions everywhere and special effects that get your heart racing. It's exciting to watch, but it is not real. This is also true of the majority of porn that is posted on the internet. It might look exciting and definitely interesting, but it isn't real.

The truth is, sex can be and is fun when it is between consenting people in a relationship, but the stuff on the internet portrays actors that are unrealistic. Many physical features of the actors and models on these porn sites are fake or enhanced to look a certain way so viewers think it's real. However, it is fiction. Fiction can serve a purpose and be entertaining, but we must remember—especially when one doesn't have their own real-life experiences to compare—that real relationships are not necessarily accurately portrayed in internet porn. When people compare themselves to the actors in porn, it can cause feelings of insecurity about their appearance and lead to unhealthy practices to try to be more like the actors and models. That's like trying to model yourself after a cartoon character—it's not real.

Another aspect about porn is that it often perpetuates violence by portraying actors/models as being victimized in one form or another. This goes against all of the values in our family and is the opposite of what sex should be: a mutually consensual experience that is not coercive, forced, or harmful. At any time, either person engaged in sexual behavior has the right to say they want to stop, and it will be honored.

When I was a kid, I felt I couldn't talk to my parents about sex because I was way too embarrassed. I want you to know you can ask Dad or me about anything, even some of the things that you've seen on the internet that confused you or made you feel uncomfortable or more curious. I know it can be difficult, awkward, and embarrassing to talk about this stuff, but you can always write me a note if that is easier. I want you to feel safe as you grow up. Sexuality is a normal part of growing up and living life. Part of my job as your parent is to make sure that we talk about the potential harms, including those posed by internet porn, so that you can make smart choices and know all of the facts.

Love always,
Mom

Now that you have learned the four steps to easing your way into a more comfortable role in your child's sexucation, you are hopefully feeling relieved, motivated, and perhaps even confident. The steps and exercises that got you to this point leave you well prepared to take action. You have all that you need to move forward with whatever it was that motivated you to read this book.

Part 3 of this book takes sexucation to an entirely new level. The remaining chapters offer a blueprint for you to organize a sex education group in your community. Whether you live in a sex-education desert or just want to create a welcoming alternative to what already exists in your community, you will find all of the details you need to form a group and share important, empowering information with youth.

Part Three

FORMING A SEX-EDUCATION GROUP FOR YOUR KIDS AND OTHER TEENS

⁕ 9 ⁕

Start Your Own Sex-Education Group

When I first offered to host a sex-education group for teens, I had not given the idea any forethought. It essentially was a leap of faith. Otherwise my brain would have taken over, and fear would have prevented me from making the offer. But in reality, I had everything I needed to create and host this group; even though I had no teaching background and only minimal group-facilitation experience, I knew I could figure out whatever came up along the way. And I was right. The group was a triumph, from both my perspective and that of the girls who participated. My main takeaway from this experience: you need not be a teacher or seasoned sex educator to lead a successful group of your own. All you need is the curiosity to learn, the willingness to lead, and the flexibility to go with the flow. To make your role easier, I offer you a road map to remove some of the guesswork.

Over the next few chapters, I'll describe my process for planning and facilitating an empowerment and discussion group for youth that is built around sex education. That way, you will see how doable this is and hopefully feel encouraged to start a group of your own. If I did it, you can too. So, let's jump in.

What Exactly Is a Girls' Group?

As I describe my process and experience, I refer to my group as "Girls' Group," or "GG," which became the default names for our group gatherings. I never bothered to change it, as I loved how naturally attendees and their parents adopted this name in our conversations, and it seemed perfectly fitting. Although my model was focused on a group of adolescents who identified as female, everyone can benefit from a group like the one described here. You can decide whom you would like to target.

Essentially, a Girls' Group is a forum for a group of friends to meet regularly and discuss a wide range of sex-education and adolescent health and well-being topics. The attendees of my Girls' Group were already friends with each other when our meetings began. This was likely a contributing factor to the group's success. (The feedback I received from the girls reiterated this.) So our two-hour meetings were not only learning opportunities for the teens. They also offered important social connections, a welcome treat at an age when such connections are so important. If you are starting your own group, consider extending an offer to teens who already know and like each other. Preexisting friendships between them will be a major incentive for them to attend.

This model was developed in direct response to the lack of a sufficient sex-ed curriculum in my local school district at the time when a group of my friends acknowledged their own discomfort with talking about sex with their daughters. It is the equivalent of the "manual" I wish I had after I opened my big mouth and volunteered to host such a group. I learned along the way, of course, but without having any point of reference. So I want to share my experience for you and other parents to model, adapt, or toss aside, as long as it gets people talking. Not only is this model a useful tool that parents can offer each other, but it is also a gift to our children. It might not be the latest gadget our tweens and teens will pine for, but its impact has greater longevity and will serve them well as they make choices throughout their lives.

The benefits of the Girls' Group model extend well beyond the education that is imparted to its participants. Here are what I consider to be the three big wins of facilitating this model:

- I had the amazing opportunity to connect with a wonderful group of girls, which brought a welcome energy and was a novelty for me because of my testosterone-filled family.

- I was excited to pick up where some of my friends felt insecure in navigating sex talks with their daughters.

- I loved offering a safe space for the girls to learn, ask, and share what was on their minds.

What makes this model unique is that it is completely accessible to all who want to replicate it. You don't have to have special credentials to start your own group. Even though I was not trained as an educator at the time (I eventually received sexuality-education certification from Planned Parenthood League of Massachusetts), I possessed and channeled something that had been with me for over three decades: the passion and desire to empower youth to make healthy decisions by providing an open, safe, and welcoming atmosphere. I knew I had what it takes to provide the girls with an enriching, informative, ongoing learning environment. And I had their parents' vote of confidence. What more did I need?

What I offer here will demystify what it takes to form a group within your own community. Together, we can work toward our shared goal: imparting important, empowering information to youth and teens on the broad subject of sex so they are prepared to make intentional, healthy decisions for themselves.

I love this model for a host of reasons. First, the topics

covered in my group were selected mainly because they were developmentally appropriate for the age of the participants, requested by the girls themselves as well as their parents, and informed by my review of several evidence-based programs that served as a loose guide for our sessions. There are so many wonderful, useful resources and curricula in existence that I didn't have to reinvent the wheel. Second, the model can be customized to address the participants' needs, and it is as flexible and as fun as you make it. Staying open and flexible is key. And don't forget to check your judgment at the door.

If you are interested in starting your own group (or multiple groups!), feel free to use this model as a template of sorts. The need for medically accurate, comprehensive sex education is immeasurable, and the more groups that are offered to fill in what is missing in schools, community settings, and homes, the better. Plus, there is no limit to the creative and fun activities you can use as teaching tools. So don't hesitate to design your own meetings that reflect your style.

The Benefits and Drawbacks of This Model

To help you decide whether to organize a sex-education group, here is a list of the pros and cons of my experience with facilitating my Girls' Group. Your list may look different from mine or another parent's. So keep in mind that what you consider to be pros might be neutral or cons for someone else and vice versa. The bottom line is that you want your list of benefits (pros) to outweigh your list of drawbacks (cons) if you want to maintain momentum for a group you form.

My List of Pros and Cons for Starting a Girls' Group	
PROS	**CONS**
• Can be done in the comfort of home • Fun • Informal; wear sweats and slippers if you like • Interactive and engaging • Convenient meeting times that work with your schedule • Adaptable to developmental stage of participants • Flexible in how much time to spend on various topics • Freedom to choose and adapt what to teach based on collective knowledge of participants • Amazing opportunity to be impactful	• Time commitment • Uncertainty about consistent attendance • What in the world will I talk about each session? • Yikes, I'm not a teacher

When I reviewed my list of cons, I realized that all but one were fear based. By asking myself what I needed to do to overcome those fears, I was able to work through them. As described in Chapter 8, our cons (or our reasons for not doing something) are perceived barriers that are surmountable when we open ourselves up to the possibilities.

PARENTAL CHALLENGE: Identifying Your Pros and Cons for Forming a Sex-Education Group

PART I

Use the space on the next page to make your own list of pros and cons. As you generate your lists, ask yourself, "What are the pros and cons of creating or facilitating a teen or tween group?" Feel free to write down your thoughts and feelings here or on a separate piece of paper, and take your time so you can be intentional as you work through this challenge.

Your List of Pros and Cons for Starting a Group	
PROS	**CONS**

PART II

Compare your lists of pros and cons above and determine which one is longer. What does this tell you about your willingness to form a sex-education group?

Next, choose one of the cons on your list and write it below.

How true is the con on a scale of 0–10, with 0 indicating "Not at All" and 10 representing "Totally, 100 percent"?

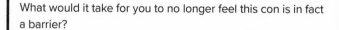

What would it take for you to no longer feel this con is in fact a barrier?

What are some options to get around this con? Get as creative as you like here.

Of the options you listed, which ones seem doable?

What small steps would help you achieve the options you feel are doable? List the baby steps you need to take for each one. Remember, no baby step is too small.

Repeat these questions for each con you jotted down.

The purpose of this Parental Challenge is to help you understand what is underneath the barrier you identified. As we talked about earlier, perceived barriers are sometimes based in fear and can be overcome. Going through this exercise may put the wheels in motion for your own group—or it may underscore the fact that you have zero interest in going down this path. If you are the latter, that is perfectly understandable. For some parents, the idea of talking to a group of adolescents about sex sounds more painful than getting a root canal. If this is you, think about who else might be interested in facilitating such a group, then bring them into the conversation to see if they are on board.

Who Do You Want to Serve?

Who needs a sex-education group? In a nutshell, everyone. Children, youth, and adults of all backgrounds can benefit from a safe group to talk about sex, sexuality, identity, consent, concerns, empowerment, and related topics. But that doesn't mean you have to open your group to the universe. The bandwidth required to serve everyone is beyond the scope of preparing to facilitate a group. The more targeted your audience, the easier it will be to offer content that resonates with your participants. This model is suitable across a variety of demographics, since it can be tailored to specific topics for your participants based on their needs. And as I said earlier, this model is a template that can be customized and used as an informal train-the-trainer.

PARENTAL CHALLENGE: Determining Your Target Group Participants

To help you zero in on your target audience, here is a brief questionnaire to encourage you to gain clarity on who you want to serve and your motivation for focusing on that population. Devote some focused time (maybe thirty minutes) to answering the following questions:

Who in the community would benefit most from participating in such a group? (Describe the age, gender identity, where they go to school, and any other specifics.)

Who do you want to serve?

What makes these individuals prime candidates for a group?

What is your motivation for wanting to organize such a group?

Why is this important?

How will participants benefit from this group?

How will the greater community benefit from this group?

Having specific criteria for the participants you want to serve is useful. It allows you to create a group with teens who are more or less at the same developmental level. For example, you may want to avoid having an age range of twelve to seventeen, which could be challenging simply because of the range of knowledge around the table and levels of maturity. Additionally, the more specific you are in defining your group, the more you can tailor the lessons according to the teens' age, grade level, gender identity, or a combination of factors.

In my case, the group found me. I had several friends whose daughters were in the midst of or on the cusp of puberty and in need of some good conversations. At the time, all six girls were friends who were in the seventh grade and either twelve or thirteen years old. As a mother of boys who sometimes feels as if she is living in a slightly calmer and modestly cleaner version of a fraternity house, I was thrilled to have the opportunity to interact with this cohort of female energy at such an incredible time in their development.

During the several years that the Girls' Group met, I received multiple requests from other local parents for their daughters to join. Unfortunately, I had to decline these requests. This was a closed group; I did not want to risk disrupting the mutual trust we had established over time. After I explained this to the other parents, they would often ask me, "Will you be starting another group any time soon? I really want my daughter to have somewhere to go." This reinforced to me that the need is there. It is everywhere, and I often told these parents that they were not alone in wanting *something* or *some way* to offer their kids the sex education they felt was missing.

You too may find a greater demand than anticipated for these groups once you start exploring the level of need. Consider pulling a few adults together—for example, some of your friends who have kids—to discuss creating and leading these sex education groups. This is a win-win, since it will reach more tweens and teens in your community while providing the facilitators a support system for sharing ideas and lessons learned. It also provides an option to broaden the participants served by having different groups by age.

A Recommendation Regarding the Group's Facilitator

It is a good idea that the facilitator of the sex-education group not have a child participating in the group. In some cases, the parent-as-group-teacher could interfere with their child's level of candidness within the group. That being said, many parent-child relationships might not create this barrier to the group dynamic, so trust your instincts when choosing a facilitator to run your group.

What Is the Goal of Your Group?

When I was preparing for my first meeting of Girls' Group, it was clear that I had the opportunity to create a fun, safe, informal learning environment. But the participants did not know what they were getting into. In fact, they did not know they were going to participate, because their parents had enlisted them during an impromptu conversation at my dinner party. The way it unfolded with the girls afterward was not a best practice of consent (one of the topics we would cover in the group, coincidentally). In my opinion, participants should be involved in the decision regarding joining a sex-education group, even if parental persuasion is exercised. Thankfully, the six girls were open and accepted the news that their moms had volunteered them for Girls' Group. In reality, the girls had the final say as to whether they wanted to participate, and I was happy that all of them were on board once they heard about the idea and that a small group of their friends would be together.

Developing a clear mission statement makes it easier to talk about the group's purpose. This is a clear, concise statement that gets everyone on the same page. There are two approaches regarding the timing of when and how a mission statement is formed, and each has its advantages:

- Craft a mission statement in advance of recruiting participants so you have it as a tool to discuss and market what you are offering and generate interest.

- Create a mission statement with participants during the first meeting as a way of getting enthusiastic for what's to come.

Both of these are viable options, and you can decide what feels best for you. Because of the spontaneous nature by which my group was formed, I drafted the mission statement—which was to "empower teens to make informed choices by providing sex education and discussions about related teen topics in a safe, open environment to foster knowledge and build communication skills"—and verbally shared it with the girls at our first meeting. In hindsight, I would have offered them an opportunity to modify it. And while it is not uncommon to revisit and adapt a mission statement as time goes by and the group evolves, our mission statement maintained its integrity for the duration of our time together.

PARENTAL CHALLENGE: Developing a Mission Statement for Your Sex-Education Group

Let's take a few moments to craft a mission statement for the group you are assembling. Here are three considerations that will drive your mission statement:

What: The purpose of the group you are forming

How: The manner in which it will be accomplished

Why: The outcome you are seeking

For my Girls' Group mission statement, I would break it down like this:

What: Empower teens to make informed choices

How: Provide sex education and discussion about related teen topics in a safe, open environment

Why: To foster knowledge and build communication skills

Now it is your turn. Use the following space to play around with a mission statement that reflects what you want for your own group. Try not to overthink it, and have some fun!

What:

How:

Why:

Put it all together to create your first draft for a mission statement:

With your mission statement options outlined, you are ready to move on to some of the logistical considerations for a successful group. The next chapter describes factors for you to ponder as you move ahead with organizing a sex-education group.

10

Logistical Considerations

t's important to consider the not-so-sexy yet practical aspects of creating and hosting your own version of a sex-education group for teens. As with any well-executed event, giving forethought to certain details in the planning stages is a necessary key step. Intentionally addressing the logistical aspects in advance of the group makes for a smoother process by eliminating a great deal of impromptu guesswork. You may still find yourself having to make unanticipated decisions that require flexibility, but having the logistics mapped out in advance will reduce this occurrence and make the setup process easier. Some of what I will cover in this chapter may feel like administrivia. However, being attentive to these details in the early planning stages will help build a strong foundation for a successful group experience.

Size

What is the ideal number of participants to include in a sex-education group? My suggestion is between six and twelve. A significant portion of a group's success is built on the collective discussion that takes place and builds on everyone's input and perspective. While a small group can offer a certain level of comfort and intimacy as well as plenty of time to get everyone's questions answered, kids may feel more on the spot because fewer participants will be in attendance. This is further magnified when someone is absent. Conversely, when a group is large, participants may enjoy feeling less pressure to speak up. A group that is too large, however, may result in some attendees clamming up and feel less inclined to actively participate.

As I mentioned in Chapter 9, my group consisted of six girls who were all in the same grade and already friends before attending Girls' Group. The fact that these girls had known each other before the group formed was a definite plus. If this is an option when you are forming your own sex-education group, I recommend exercising it. Getting adolescent friends together is an additional incentive to regular attendance, and that is gold for a facilitator.

Scheduling

With the varied schedules of your family members, planning anything can become tricky. Landing on a time that works for a group facilitator and the attendees is no different. One of my measures of a successful group is the attendance record. Do participants show up? What prevents them from attending? In our Girls' Group, which was small, we couldn't afford to lose more than two participants at a given meeting without altering the group's dynamics. Therefore, consider how to accommodate the schedules of your participants to effectively maximize attendance.

Getting meeting times on everyone's calendar can make this easier. To some extent in middle school, and to a great degree in high school, finding a regular time to gather is a bigger challenge than you would expect. Between sports, extracurricular activities, homework, family events, and job responsibilities, carving out time for yet another activity requires flexibility. Initially, scheduling was done through the parents. Once the girls entered high school, I took the parents out of the scheduling loop. This was an intentional move on my part to help the girls "own" the responsibility of managing their calendar. This was easier than you might think as it became apparent that attending group meetings was *their* priority, and the girls would schedule things around Girls' Group, to the extent that they could. Our group landed on weekend afternoons, typically Sundays. Remaining flexible as to the exact time of the meeting was critical to accommodating unbreakable commitments, and on rare occasions, one person would have to miss a meeting. At the conclusion of each meeting, as everyone slowly cleaned up any snacks and finished catching up with each other, I would interrupt and confirm the date and time of the next meeting.

Another approach would be to have a fixed time when the group meets. For example, setting the meetings for the third Sunday of the month from three to five thirty would eliminate scheduling the next meeting at the end of every prior meeting. This approach may be easier for groups with more participants. The bottom line, however, is to choose the approach that feels best to you and/or the facilitator.

Frequency of Meetings

There is no magic answer for how often you should convene your sexucation meetings. Here are a few questions to guide you as you make a plan for your sessions:

- What is the goal of your group?
- How will you achieve this?
- How long will that take?
- What is your availability to facilitate these meetings? If someone else is the facilitator, what is their availability?

These are certainly broad questions, but they will prompt you to think about running a sex-education group for X number of meetings over Y number of months. It is reasonable to set aside time for a minimum of eight meetings and spread them out over a schedule that feels comfortable for you (weekly, biweekly, etc.). In my case, I originally thought I would convene GG for six to eight meetings to cover what I deemed to be the biggest gaps in the local school district's sex-education curriculum. However, as the group quickly gelled and we found our stride, other topics organically came up that lent themselves to additional meetings. Since we had the flexibility to meet beyond the timeframe I had originally allotted, we kept going . . . and going . . . and going. Five years later, we ended the group several weeks before the girls graduated from high school. By then, the frequency of the meetings had decreased, since we had already covered a large breadth of material and it was hard to pinpoint meeting dates when the majority of the group was available. However, because of the bond that had formed, it made sense to continue (albeit less often) for as long as we did.

Length of Meetings

Keeping your group engaged and engrossed is another factor for success. One ingredient for this is keeping the meeting length to the "just right" amount of time, which is the point just before participants lose interest or become distracted by thoughts of homework, social plans with friends, and other obligations. There is no magic answer for the perfect meeting length, given that each person's ability to focus on what's in front of them differs. So the length of the meeting should allow time for whatever topic the facilitator intends to cover, while maintaining engagement and respect for the teens' busy lives. Being able to read the room and inspire engagement will serve the group well.

Flexibility is key. If your objective is to maximize engagement, keep the meetings to within ninety minutes. Even if there is a great deal of material to cover, participants lead busy lives and have other commitments that they will need to tend to. Additionally, it is better to end while the energy level is still high, rather than running everyone to the point where they are tired and lose interest. Some meetings may conclude early. Others may run over by minutes to an hour, depending on what is on the meeting agenda and if the group is available to stay longer. Thus, maintaining openness and flexibility while reading the room will become easier as the group gels. It will also serve you well as an effective facilitator.

Meeting Location

Another factor for success is the accessibility of the meetings. Are they easy to get to? Is the space warm and welcoming? There are a number of options to consider for housing the meetings, ranging from various community spaces to someone's home. I opted to hold meetings at my house since it was centrally located and accessible to all participants, as well as cost-free. Most of the girls lived within easy walking distance of my house, the others a short car ride away. Plus, I prefer using a home to convene the meetings if the size of the group allows it. The casual and inviting feeling afforded by meeting at home created an environment that put participants at ease. It also enabled me to use different spaces within the house depending on what I had planned for the meeting. We most often sat around the dining room table. Occasionally, we gathered in the family room, where we had a big-screen television for the rare times we watched a video or film for discussion.

As the meetings were held in my home, I followed a strict policy that no one from my family could be home during Girls' Group. I wanted a sacred space for our group so no one felt inhibited to talk. This meant that the members of my family got booted from the home a couple of times per month. This was easy enough to do, though it would occasionally require creative planning. On a couple of occasions, I had to adapt the meetings due to conflicting schedules within my family. For example, my youngest son was home for two or three meetings due to circumstances beyond my control. So I gave him noise-cancelling headphones and a movie to watch on my computer behind closed doors and on a different floor of the house. Then, at the beginning of the meeting, I informed the girls that my son was home and told them where he was and what he was doing. I then received their consent to proceed. I never wanted to give the girls a reason to distrust me, and they met my transparency about the circumstances with openness.

In addition to having a space where participants were free to speak candidly, I wanted to create an environment that felt warm and welcoming. A few years ago, I discovered the concept of hygge (pronounced hue-ga), the Danish word to describe a setting that is warm, cozy, simple, and comforting. Often, hygge is associated with informal gatherings with friends over nourishing food and drink with less focus on the presentation and greater emphasis on the togetherness. These elements all help to produce warm, fuzzy feelings that fill our souls with the enjoyment of simple pleasures. It also gave a name to something I'd been practicing for years without realizing it. Although I did not adhere to my usual hygge standard for the Girls' Group meetings, I recognized the importance of creating an inviting space and borrowed from the concept to create an ambience that enabled the girls to feel at ease and settle into each discussion.

Meeting Structure

As the group facilitator, you have the creative leeway to structure the meetings in a manner that works best for you as well as the participants. If it's doable, have the group sit together around a table. Sitting in a circle in a room that has comfortable seating—such as couches, chairs, and floor cushions—works nicely too. This will maximize participation and engagement within the group. Avoid structuring the meeting in a way that resembles a classroom to set it apart from school. A less formal and more comfortable environment is in keeping with the purpose of the group.

Having a predictable flow for the meetings is helpful, since it helps the teens know what to expect each time. A routine about how the meeting will unfold is comforting. Additionally, an agenda provides the framework for that day's topics of discussion. Meanwhile, varying the kinds of activities within the meetings will maintain participants' interest and keep the gatherings more fun. This combination of predictability and variation adds to the group's appeal. Below is an example of the schedule I followed for the majority of Girls' Group meetings:

- 4:00: Arrival (grab hot beverage and get seated at table)
- 4:10: Check-in (everyone has an opportunity to share how they are)
- 4:20: Introduce topic of the week
- 4:40: Topic-related exercise or game
- 5:00: Interactive discussion
- 5:10: Q & A

- 5:25: Distribution of index cards and question prompt for the anonymous box

It is a good idea to vary the activities from meeting to meeting, since it will help capture and maintain the participants' interest. For example, one week I would show a brief video and use it as a springboard for discussion. Another week I would include an exercise fashioned after a game show, followed by a lively discussion about the experience and what the girls learned from it. Occasionally we would watch a feature-length film and discuss it for twenty to thirty minutes afterward (or at the following meeting, if we ran short on time). For these movie-oriented meetings, we would move to the family room and comfortably arrange ourselves on the large sectional couch with our snacks and warm beverages. Again, flexibility is key. This includes being open to participants leaving before a meeting is over.

The Fun Stuff

Some logistics are rather fun to plan and offer opportunities for creativity. In this section, I share how I addressed three logistical areas, keeping it fun and playful. You may have your own creative ideas and are invited to use yours or modify mine in a manner that feels best to you.

The Attraction of Snacks

Surprise! Food incentivizes participation among kids and adults alike. I have noticed that my interest in a meeting is piqued when the prospect of a meal, baked goods, or even a decent cup of coffee is waved in front of me. And I lost track of the number of times when, during my previous corporate life, I fell for the lure of food at optional learn-in meetings. Thanks to the persuasion of a tasty alternate to the sad leftovers I had brought from home, I expanded my knowledge base on corporate issues I would never have otherwise learned about. Maybe this resonates with you, and you can recall meetings or events that drew you in with similar enticements.

Applying this theory to Girls' Group, I ensured that snacks were an intentional aspect of every gathering. My standard offering was simple and inexpensive: hot tea and two or three snacks, with both sweet and savory options available. A hot kettle of water would greet the girls upon arrival so they could grab a mug and pour themselves a cup of tea or cocoa. Then we would gather around the dining room table where the snacks awaited. These details might sound mundane, but they helped make the routine inviting and cozy and allowed the girls to gently transition from wherever they had come from and settle in. The girls also appreciated whatever food I offered. Sometimes they would arrive ravenous, having had no time for proper refueling before the meeting.

From time to time, the girls would come to our meetings with a home-baked snack or other food to share. Distributing this responsibility with a rotating schedule of who is assigned to bring snacks is an option to consider when you organize your own group. This encourages the participants to share the responsibility and expense while relieving the host or facilitator of carrying this task exclusively.

Folders for Notes and Handouts

Before your group's first meeting, it is a good idea to purchase a two-pocket folder for each participant and include blank paper in each one. This is where the teens can store any handouts and notes they keep from each meeting. A fun activity at one of the early meetings can be to have the participants decorate their folders with items you provide, such as stickers, markers, or items to make their own aspirational collages. Then, at the end of each meeting, collect the folders and securely store them for the participants. This way, they do not have to remember to bring them to each meeting or fear that someone at home might rifle through their materials.

The Anonymous Box

During our Girls' Group meetings, I would place a lidded

box approximately the size of a small shoebox in the center of the table. Then I would give each girl three index cards to anonymously write down any questions or statements "as needed" and put them in the box. Finally, at the end of each meeting, I would ask a thought-provoking question and require that everyone write down a response, no matter how relevant they felt it was to their personal life circumstances. That way, all of the girls would submit at least one card per meeting. This routine was incredibly useful and drove many subsequent discussions on topics that participants had indicated on their index cards. You may have experience participating in similar anonymous Q&A sessions and know just how useful it is at eliciting feedback from all participants. I encourage you to use your own anonymous box as a safe and confidential way to collect input from your meeting participants.

* 11 *

Group Dynamics

This chapter addresses three items that are key to building a respectful, cohesive group. Whether participants have preexisting friendships or are new to each other, fruitful discussions will involve input from everyone. The self-consciousness that is prevalent during the teen years can act as an obstacle to active participation in meetings, but it can be overcome by creating a safe and solid container for discussions. Starting with the first meeting, it is important to establish ground rules, build trust, and keep it engaging. Building a strong foundation for the group relationship goes a long way and sets the tone for the journey together. I observed that my group became more forthcoming as time went on, a factor I attribute to their becoming more comfortable with me.

Establishing Ground Rules

Laying out the ground rules for your sex-education group is an important early step that will make the policies and rules that drive the group clear to everyone. This is imperative given the sensitive subjects that will be addressed and the need to maintain confidentiality within the group. However, it does not have to be the first step. I prefer to address rules and policies after breaking the ice and having a bit of fun to put everyone at ease. Having clearly defined ground rules will ensure that respect and confidentiality are maintained, and it will create a container that enables all participants to feel safe and speak openly without concern of judgment, disrespect, or gossip.

At our first Girls' Group meeting, I distributed copies of our group's ground rules to each girl. We then went around the table, taking turns reading the rules aloud until all of the bullets were read. Here are those rules, for you to use or adapt:

- A person's unique qualities are to be celebrated

- Everyone is entitled to talk and be taken seriously

- No one will be required to speak if they do not want to

- Participants are tasked with learning as much as they can about themselves, which includes receiving honest answers to honest questions

- Everything said in the group will remain confidential

- We agree to keep the details of what is said in the group

among ourselves. We may talk about meetings outside of the group in general terms (e.g., *Today we talked about what consent means and looks like*), but we will not mention specifics that include names (e.g., *Mary said that she was afraid to tell Chris she didn't want to become more sexual with him because . . .*).

- We agree to keep anything that occurs between group members to ourselves. We understand that there is an exception to this confidentiality, which applies to the group leader *only* if the group leader believes that someone is in danger. The leader has a professional obligation to take direct action in order to keep everyone safe.

- We agree that the group leader has to follow the same confidentiality procedures as the participants, will not share the details of the group meetings with others except in the most general terms, and will not use names of individuals in the group.

- No group member is ever required to answer any questions or participate in any activity they do not want to. We all agree not to pressure anyone to participate in any discussion or activity after that person has passed or refused. We understand the group leader is obligated to protect this right.

- Gossip and secret grudges can be very destructive in a group. We agree that if you have something to say to another group member, you will say it directly to the member in the safety of the group, using respectful language, rather than behind her back.

Building Trust

Trust is one of the most important building blocks for good relationships. I knew that if I was going to be an effective facilitator and have a successful group, I would need to earn the girls' trust. It also wouldn't hurt for the girls, who had known each other for years by this point, to learn about the group process and understand the importance of trust in the sacred container of Girls' Group. Earning their trust was necessary if they were going to listen, participate, and feel safe in the group. Since I had known their families for a few years and my older son had become friends with most of the girls through school, I was entering this situation with a degree of familiarity. However, I knew it was imperative to establish trust because of our overlapping social circles. I was determined to do what I needed to establish a healthy, confidential, trustworthy rapport with them that was independent of our connections.

In an effort to keep things fun, I kicked off my trust-building campaign by using some reliably fun icebreakers. These activities and games are multipurpose in that they achieve the following:

- They are fully inclusive, engaging each participant equally.

- They invite people to share things about themselves that may not be common knowledge (e.g., that I used to place my sacred security blanket over my head when I was four years old while watching my favorite PBS show, *Zoom*, pretending it was the long hair I wished I had, just like one of the hosts I so admired).

- They build rapport. I did not fool myself into believing that a single icebreaker would be the magic formula that instantly dissolved whatever guards the girls and I were holding onto, but I knew it was an important first step.

- They create a positive atmosphere and inviting learning environment.

I love icebreakers for the fun and laughter they can produce as well as the trust they build. So as a facilitator who wanted to earn the trust of the group, it was important to participate openly and fully as one of the group members, thus giving myself a wonderful opportunity to reveal my own vulnerability and model openness and non-judgment. In hindsight, I realize I shared things with the girls that I had never stated aloud before, yet it seemed perfectly natural in the setting we created.

I will never forget when my eldest son, who was twelve at the time, walked past me as I was busy preparing my plans for the first Girls' Group meeting on my laptop. He had already declared himself the authority on what would constitute a successful Girls' Group, and that day he warned, "You better make it fun."

"What do you mean?" I asked.

"Don't get too serious or anything. Just play games."

Actually, I was already a couple of steps ahead of my sage boy. Games comprised half of my agenda for our first meeting. I knew I couldn't launch into a presentation about what it means to feel empowered, or (gasp) talk about intimate topics such as transforming bodies, sexual pleasure, and discharge without establishing safety and mutual trust. Building trust with some fun icebreakers was going to be key if I wanted to engage these girls in fruitful group discussions later on. And besides promoting group cohesiveness and reinforcing respect for our differences, icebreakers would give me an excuse to dole out candy, which is always a crowd-pleaser. (Non-food rewards such as fun trinkets, cool stickers, colorful paper clips, uninflated balloons, and crayons work well too, especially if you want to avoid giving the teens sugar.)

The first icebreaker I used required Skittles. Yes, it was

imperative that I had these or other multicolored candies (Starbursts, M&M's, Jolly Ranchers, etc.) stocked and hidden in my house so my family didn't eat my stash. At the first Girls' Group meeting, I placed a bowl of the candy in the center of the table and instructed the girls to take three Skittles, each one a different color. Once everyone had selected theirs, I explained that we would go around the table and talk about ourselves based on the Skittles we had chosen using the following talking prompts:

- Green: Tell us something we do not know about you.
- Red: Tell us about one of your favorite books.
- Purple: Tell us something you are good at.
- Yellow: Share a fear or concern you have.
- Orange: Describe an embarrassing moment you experienced.

At first, the girls reacted to the instructions with giggles and uncomfortable looks. But once we started the exercise, it sparked great conversations, and we had a blast. And after we finished going around the table and sharing our three facts, I invited the girls to enjoy the rest of the candy bowl's contents throughout the meeting.

One of the beauties of this particular icebreaker is how

flexible and adaptable it is. As the facilitator, you can determine in advance your own talking prompts as well as how many pieces of candy (or other desired items) you want each participant to take. The prompts should cover a range of areas, though. Some prompts will be easier to respond to than others. Yet all of them will provide opportunities for you and the participants to engage in conversations and start building trust.

I have included a few of my favorite icebreakers at the end of the book. Dozens—if not hundreds—more are available on the internet. You may have a few favorites already. No matter what, you get to decide which icebreakers feel appropriate given the mission and size of the group you're facilitating.

Engaging Your Participants

The key to engagement is twofold. It is both content driven and activity driven. The next chapter offers suggestions for topics that can be customized according to a variety of factors. For now, let's focus on maximizing engagement so you can build on my experience in a manner that feels comfortable to you. Because, let's face it: the idea of organizing, preparing for, and facilitating a group like the one I have been describing can sound intimidating. If you do not have a background in teaching or group work, this might feel even scarier. And it makes sense that it is even more daunting given the topic at hand, which, as we've already established, is uncomfortable for so many parents. The exercises and encouragement I offer in the list below are intended to eliminate that discomfort and help you realize that you have what it takes to lead your own group.

- **Engage all participants.** Some participants may dominate the talking space, while others will shy away from it. Manage the room the best you can. Ideally, you want to keep any one individual from dominating the air space. Consider asking questions such as "Does anyone else have something to add?" to draw out the more reserved participants. Activities that provide them a moment for reflection or writing down their thoughts before sharing may also help even out the talking space.

- **Converse instead of lecturing.** As it will be necessary to lead a discussion with facts and information, ensure there is room built in for questions and comments or activities related to the topic.

- **Ask a topic-related question.** Encourage participants to share their answers out loud, and go around the table for responses. This will help everyone focus on the day's subject at the beginning of the meeting.

- **Stay on topic.** Occasionally, a participant will get off topic, and before you know it, the conversation has gone in a completely different direction. Do not be afraid to reel in your participants. You can always ask that person to jot down their thoughts about the unrelated topic. Then, if there is time at the end of the meeting, you can revisit the side topic as a group.

- **Use "we" instead of "you."** This will prevent individual participants from feeling called out for expressing their opinions. For example, "It sounds like we feel _____ about _____."

- **Avoid putting participants on the defensive.** Instead of asking "Why?" which can put people on the spot, dig deeper on issues of interest using questions like "Can anyone tell me more about this?" that the whole group can respond to.

- **Restate what you are hearing.** That way, you can ensure that you've correctly understood what a participant has said.

- **Wrap up the discussion.** Summarize the big concepts and discussion points.

As I've said before, this model for sex-education groups is so replicable, and its adaptability makes it user-friendly. Our communities need more courageous facilitators—parents, guardians, grandparents, and other trusted adults—to step forward. There is no shortage of discussion topics and resources that can be customized to fit the particular needs of your newly formed group. In fact, you can check out some of my go-to resources in the Resources section at the end of the book.

Finally, to emphasize something I stressed in earlier chapters, the need for groups for all tweens and teens, regardless of gender identity, is absolutely critical. As a parent of two sons, I recognize that all of our children need comprehensive sex education in an environment where they are comfortable and free to be themselves. All humans have the right to information that helps them live healthfully and make choices based on facts. What I share about the Girls' Group model I created is not gender specific and can be used and modified for any group that you convene. So if you choose to create your own sex-education group, definitely consider collaborating with other parents to ensure your group meets the needs of your family as well as your community.

12

Subjects to Cover in Your Group

There are oodles of books, programs, and other educational resources with up-to-date information to guide you on your sexucation journey. Whether you decide to host a recurring group or are planning to up your game in the conversations you have within your own family, consider the breadth and depth of what you discuss. The conversations that you initiate can build on existing resources that reinforce positive attitudes and beliefs while building skills that promote healthy behaviors.

When assessing resources to use as educational tools, be mindful of when the material was created and who created or sponsored it. The first factor—when the material was created—is important because, while much of sexucation is timeless, a great deal of information has evolved over the last few decades and continues to change at a rapid pace. Being up-to-date on topics ranging from contraceptive methods to inclusion of LGBTQ+ identity and rights is critical in facilitating a useful and meaningful sex-education group that resonates with youth today.

The second factor—knowing who created or sponsored a resource you are considering—is important for understanding the motivation behind it. For example, some religious groups and conservative organizations that publish sex-education materials omit key factual information to promote a specific agenda. This may be evident from reading a description of the educational resource. In other cases, it may be intentionally subtle in order to attract a wider audience and then withhold certain facts or possibly share misinformation to support the organization's beliefs. Reading the book covers and flaps and skimming through the pages or online resource will give you a sense of the larger purpose of that resource. If it is not obvious, a quick internet search of the author/organization who published it will help identify if there is an alternate agenda. Having this awareness allows you to be intentional in promoting the factual information you want to cover in your group.

One of the beautiful benefits of being involved in your child's sex education is the opportunity to impart your family's values while sharing important facts. This is one of the gifts of being the primary educator. As a group facilitator to a broader audience than your own child, you can ensure that the discussion will be less value-laden and more focused on comprehensive, factual, medically accurate information.

Remaining value neutral when you are acting as facilitator can be challenging. To illustrate this further, imagine that your son's teacher, while teaching a particular subject, imposes her biases on the discussion—biases that conflict with values that are important to your family. Her opinions are not relevant to the factual material being taught and therefore do not contribute to the lesson.

When hosting a group, keep in mind that participants will undoubtedly arrive with varied levels of baseline knowledge, whether they openly admit it or not. This means that whatever lessons you have prepared may be new information to all the participants and other times a review for some individuals or the whole group. The interactive nature of this model, with the use of worksheets, games, and other creative ways of involving everyone, organically encourages participation, regardless of previous knowledge level. As a result, this group model feels like a social gathering where information is imparted, rather than a traditional learning environment. This kind of learning is fun and informal.

Also, it is a good idea to hold off on diving into content until after the first group meeting. Instead, use the first gathering to establish rapport, set the stage for what's to come in upcoming meetings, and most of all, have fun. For example, the goal I established for my first GG meeting was not to focus on subject matter, but rather to get the girls talking and laughing as well as establish ground rules and the group's mission while building connection.

Topics for Discussion

By now, you likely understand that what is offered in this book are suggestions rather than a prescription. You are free to pick from the list of topics below based on the information gaps you feel exist in your community's sex-education programs or, more specifically, among your group participants or family. Adapting the discussion to fit the needs of your audience according to where they are in their sexucation is up to you. The topics I introduced in my GG were intended to provide factual information, empower participants, promote healthy attitudes about self and sexuality, and be inclusive of all sexual and gender identities and expressions. I wanted to avoid fear-based tactics and instead create a safe space for the girls to explore additional topics of their choice. Initially, I intended to focus only on sexual health topics. However, we ultimately covered so much more.

Within each of these topics are many categories to explore. This list is not exhaustive; it is simply the one I generated, and there may be holes in what is covered here. If you do not see a particular sex-education topic listed below, check out the Resources section at the end of the book for organizations, websites, and publications that may help you.

Abstinence
This refers to one's decision to refrain from sexual behaviors. Many people are surprised to learn that abstinence is included in comprehensive sex education.

Access to Services
It is one thing to know the theoretical information about what to do when particular needs for X, Y, and Z arise; it is another thing altogether to identify where, in particular, needed resources and services are available within one's geographic reach. This will vary greatly depending on where one resides (rural, urban, suburban) and the overall political and religious beliefs that dominate the area.

Alcohol, Drugs, and Impact on Decisions
Although, for the most par, consuming alcohol and drugs is illegal in the United States until age twenty-one, many kids will participate in consumption well before they are of legal age. Understanding the physiological, emotional, and decision-making impact while under the influence serves to educate youth to stay safe.

Body Image

Having a positive body image is a challenge at any age, and even more so during adolescence when there is a tendency to compare oneself to peers and media influencers. A positive body image is feeling comfortable and confident in your body without obsessing about looking a certain way. In contrast, negative body image may be based on distorted perceptions of one's physique and involves feeling uncomfortable in one's body. Negative body image can be linked to low self-esteem, eating disorders, and a host of other challenges. Discussions that raise awareness about factors that contribute to one's body image and strategies to overcome negative influences are particularly useful.

Boundaries, Consent, and Communication

Sexual boundaries vary not only from person to person, but from moment to moment. Consent is an ongoing process between intimate partners. Clear, unambiguous communication is important to ensure that individuals' boundaries are respected and the possibility of assumptions and misunderstandings is eliminated.

Bullying

Bullying is a repeated behavior designed to inflict harm on the target. It shows up in many different forms: physical, verbal, emotional, and cyber. Understanding why some people bully, ways of dealing with bullying, and putting a stop to it are important life skills.

Contraception

There are many birth control options available today, from abstinence to condoms to long-acting, reversible contraceptives (e.g., IUDs, implants), pills, patches, shots, and many more. The ease of use, duration of use, and effectiveness vary. Understanding the pros and cons of each method is valuable in educating people about their options so they can make a choice that is right for them. People's needs change over time, so what feels like the best option for an individual at one point in their lives can change.

Gender and Sexual Identities and Expression

Although the gamut of sexual and gender identities and expressions has existed since the beginning of humanity, positive inclusion of this topic has been left out of health education until relatively recently. Myopic categorizations used in the past have expanded to reach a broader base of the population so that everyone is included, not only those individuals that fall within a binary male/female, straight/gay classification. Inclusion is critical so that all people feel seen, validated, and accepted.

Healthy Outlets

There are a variety of coping mechanisms people turn to when they are stressed or upset. Awareness of healthy vs. unhealthy choices and how to channel the energy into healthy habits are lifelong skills that adolescents are well situated to learn.

Healthy Relationships

Respect, trust, honoring boundaries, mutual consent, and communication skills are but some of the components of a healthy relationship. Empowering teens to embrace these factors and understand that no one should accept an unhealthy relationship is key. Identifying trusted adults—a parent, aunt, uncle, older sibling, friend's parent, etc.—is helpful, as teens benefit from having someone they can talk to about relationship concerns.

Media Literacy

From print ads to porn, learning how to interpret what is real and what is manipulated is an important skill that serves people of all ages.

Moods

Mood swings are a common occurrence in adolescence and can be disconcerting to the individual experiencing them. Creating self-awareness of moods and emotions and understanding what, if anything, triggers them is a useful tool to manage them in healthy ways.

Peer Pressure

Social acceptance drives a lot of human behavior. But what happens when it conflicts with our values, and we really do not want to conform? Bringing this internal conflict to light gives strength to one's resolve. Strategies to avoid peer pressure can make it easier to avoid participating in an unwanted activity.

Pleasure

Sexual feelings, thoughts, and desires are natural drivers of pleasure-seeking, consensual physical touch. Self-pleasure (masturbation) is also a normal part of healthy human sexuality. Not only is masturbation safe, but it also helps individuals understand what feels good and have autonomy over their sexuality.

Pregnancy Options

Pregnancy sometimes happens unplanned. Understanding the options one has (parenting, adoption, abortion) is important in making decisions that fit best with an individual based on personal factors.

Puberty

This covers not only the physical changes that occur during the process of puberty but also the changes that take place emotionally and developmentally. Whereas you may recall the nuts-and-bolts lessons from biology class when you were growing up, there are amazing opportunities to weave in discussions about new or unexpected feelings, changes in friendships or interests, moodiness, and other new feelings. It's important to explain that these experiences are normal during this phase of incredible development.

Reproduction

Curricula of the past focused on the post-pubescent physically mature male and female bodies and how they work together to reproduce. In updated material, other means of reproduction that extend well beyond male–female vaginal penetration are part of the discussion. There are myriad ways in which people today grow their families, families including but not limited to same-sex couples, individuals, and heterosexuals experiencing infertility.

Safer Sex

"Safer sex" describes what you can do to protect yourself and your partner from STIs. Some sexual behaviors carry greater risks, and understanding the options available to reduce the risk of transmission is an important step for anyone who is thinking about being physically intimate with someone.

Sexually Transmitted Infections and HIV

There are numerous bacterial and viral infections that are spread through sexual contact. Many people who have them do not have any symptoms. This can lead to serious health problems. Learning the different types of infections, how they can be prevented, long-term health risks, and the importance of getting tested and treated is necessary to encourage overall health.

Stress

Adolescence is a stressful time because of various factors, including school, friends, family, work, sports, illness, and many other issues that tweens and teens may face. Acknowledging that stress is a normal part of this time in their lives and identifying healthy coping strategies can help ease some of the discomfort that stress can induce.

Touch

There are different kinds of touch: nurturing, affectionate, sexual, violent, exploitative, and so on. Understanding the differences between them is a large topic in itself. This can also serve as a natural springboard for a discussion about consent.

PARENTAL CHALLENGE: Zeroing in on What to Cover in Your Group

As a group organizer/facilitator, you get to plan the initial topics to be covered in the group. As described earlier, this can evolve over time based on the input provided by participants. For baseline planning purposes, answer the following questions to help you zero in on subjects to cover in your sex-education group.

In reviewing the above list of sex-education topics, what is your first reaction?

Which topics feel easier to discuss?

Which topics feel more challenging to discuss? Why?

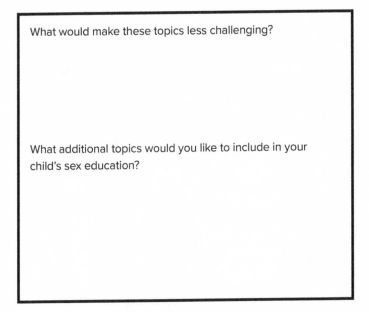

What would make these topics less challenging?

What additional topics would you like to include in your child's sex education?

With so many amazing topics to discuss, it can feel over-whelming to jump on board. Having a comprehensive list can make it hard to figure out where to begin. The good news is, you get to choose! There is no single correct way or order in which to introduce material, though some topics will feel more natural to discuss after others as they build on each other. And even though some topics may feel more challenging to broach based on your personal level of com-fort, the previous chapters, including the Parental Challenge exercises, and *practice* make you well prepared to create a successful comprehensive sex-education group.

The Impact of Girls' Group, in Their Own Words

Ever the researcher who wants to evaluate and refine what exists, I asked the participants of Girls' Group to reflect on their experience and offer insight about what worked and what could be improved. Their valuable feedback may be useful for informing your decisions about similar groups you may organize. The highlights of their responses are summarized below.

If you were going to tell a friend about Girls' Group (GG), how would you describe it?

- "GG taught us comprehensive sex ed and generally helped us with the transition into adolescence, from middle to high school."

- "Girls' Group was a tight-knit group of friends who got together weekly or biweekly to talk about difficult subjects, including peer pressure, sex, and drugs with a person who they felt comfortable talking to in a space that felt safe."

- "Girls' Group became my safe learning space to ask questions and learn about the changes that were occurring with our bodies and our lives . . . Girls' Group was an environment in which I felt safe asking questions. Since I was surrounded by my closest friends, it allowed us to connect in new ways and not feel awkward around topics that usually made me uncomfortable."

- "I actually just recently told a friend about it! I described it as a way for young women to gain useful information about their bodies, gender, and sexuality. I also described it as 'the health class we should have been offered in high school.' I believe it assisted me in understanding the importance of feeling comfortable in my own body at a somewhat confusing stage in life."

- "I would describe Girls' Group as a place where you won't feel judged for anything you share—somewhere you can forget about things that are stressing you out in life."

- "A group of young girls actively discussing the physical and emotional process of getting older."

How did Girls' Group benefit you?

- "The biggest benefit came not from the things I learned but instead from the values GG imbued in me. I am open to talking about and learning about sex and sexuality, and thanks to GG I know that when it comes to those there is no normal. I feel incredibly lucky to have learned this because people that maintain prejudice toward perceived differences just serve to perpetuate hate. I feel as though GG has enabled me to challenge norms through teaching me that differences are not only okay but are welcomed."

- "GG was especially helpful in middle school when kids were just beginning to become exposed to certain words, actions, and ideas. I have always struggled to talk about more personal subjects. GG was a place for me to ask questions without feeling judged or without receiving some kind of lecture as a response. It was also incredibly beneficial to be in this environment with friends you've known for years and to hear them talk about similar problems and/or give advice about how to handle certain situations. I was incredibly lucky to have a group of people I felt supported by and felt comfortable sharing so much without consequence (what is said in GG stays in GG)."

- "Girls' Group gave me knowledge about sex education that I would never receive in school. It also gave me a safe space to talk about the changes going on in our lives."

- "Girls' Group taught me how to be comfortable in my own body. It better prepared me for the parts of life nobody really ever talks to you about when you're a young adult. Although I was initially hesitant about joining and being a part of Girls' Group, I will forever be grateful for what it taught me."

- "Girls' Group benefitted me by making me feel not as alone, and it also helped me realize that pretty much all of the problems I was facing were not abnormal."

What did you like best about Girls' Group?

- "It was very important that it was led by a woman who was not my mother, because we often discussed things that would've been uncomfortable to discuss with my own mom. It allowed me to not only open up personally but also to be more receptive to the information I was receiving. It felt like such a safe space every time we met, which was so great."

- "I liked the camaraderie; I liked knowing that at least once a week we would be together. Something I loved about our friend group was how independent we all were and how much our interests and passions differed. The catch-up session at the beginning of each meeting was always much needed and fun."

- "I liked the anonymous question/suggestion box set out for us in the middle of the table. If anyone had any questions they weren't comfortable asking directly, or any conversation they wanted to have but were hesitant to initiate, they were welcome to write it down and slip it in the box without any questions being asked. The question or comment would then come up anonymously, and as a result we were able to have a more open and judgment-free discussion."

- "I also loved when Andrea would ask a question and we'd go around in a circle providing our answers and insights. I loved listening to what the others had to say, because very often each gave a completely different, yet valid and relevant, answer. I was astonished by how much I learned from them and how much more I got to know them as friends, students, girls, and people."

- "I really appreciated how everything in Girls' Group stayed in Girls' Group. There was no judgment, and we could have educated discussions."

- "I loved being able to see close friends, especially in between busy school weeks when we may not have had the time to hang out otherwise. It was nice to be able to discuss topics that most people feel are uncomfortable to talk about. We were definitely close to begin with, but this seemed to bring us closer, offering us a safe and caring space to learn about each other and our bodies."

- "Even though we were all friends, I feel like I am pretty reserved and do not really talk about myself. I liked how Girls' Group made me feel very safe, and I started to not have a problem with sharing my thoughts. It helped that we were all friends, but even in groups with unfamiliar people I come out of my shell the more we interact."

- "I liked the people I was surrounded by. It made everything feel very safe and open."

What would have made GG better?

- "I think we made the best of the time we had, and I am so grateful for this unique experience. Towards the end we weren't able to meet as frequently as we grew up and grew out of old routines, establishing new ones in high school. I wish we had met more toward the end of high school, but more so to just talk and catch up rather than working through the curriculum."

- "I wish I had experienced more of the things we talked about while we were talking about them. Now, as a college sophomore, I have experienced several of the subjects we talked about and am so relieved to have the information that I gained from this group in the back of my mind."

- "I think that if we were able to have these types of discussions and education in school, then it would have enhanced Girls' Group so much more, making it something that we didn't want to keep secretive because it was normalized in our society."

- "I do not think I would have changed anything about GG. I honestly looked forward to it each week!"

- "I think it would have been cool to go on some field trips here and there, or maybe even just outside for a change of scenery."

How do you think other adolescents could benefit from GG (or any similar group regardless of gender identity)?

- "I think all adolescents could benefit from a group such as this one. Even if their high school does have a comprehensive sex-ed program (ours certainly did not), there is so much value in meeting in a small group setting with people you are comfortable with rather than a classroom setting with classmates. With all the formative changes that occur throughout adolescent years, it can feel really isolating, but having a group like GG that is a safe place to talk about those changes serves as a reminder that other people are also going through the same things, which is very comforting."

- "I believe a group like this could be valuable to so many people regardless of gender identity or age. However, I think that one of the main reasons for our group's success was that we were friends, close friends. I'm not sure I would have been able to open up the way I did as quickly as I did around strangers or even acquaintances. But that's just me. I can imagine that there are people who would rather have these kinds of conversations around people who know less about them than their friends who they see every day (who might judge them, leak information, etc.). A huge part of the group's effectiveness is reliant on the prevailing social dynamic."

- "I think everybody should have somebody they feel they can talk to about anything without consequence. Many young people do not receive helpful information about topics (e.g., sex, drugs) that could have significant and lasting effects on their social and personal lives until it's too late. I think one of the aims of GG was to tackle these issues before they arose so they could be handled maturely in the moment."

- "I definitely think that Girls' Group can help all adolescents. Observing my younger sibling go through school with no sex education worries me, because this information is important and needs to be public knowledge. The platform of Girls' Group is to normalize sex education and allow openness of conversations in the lives of teenagers."

- "I learned more from Girls' Group about myself and the way my body works than from any high school health class I had taken. I didn't quite realize the lack of information being taught until Girls' Group! My hope is that every young adolescent is offered a form of Girls' Group, whether it be a health class with better and more defined curriculum, or a group like ours."

- "I think it's super important for adolescents to have that connection with people. During your adolescent years, you typically feel misunderstood by your parents and feel like no one knows what you are feeling. Groups like Girls' Group are literally having discussions with your peers about life and things you might be angry about. Having people that understand as well as a neutral adult that really listens to you is so helpful when you are moving through rough stages in life. I think it also would help your relationship with your parents, because you have that neutral adult that will try to help you understand your parents' point of view and realize that they are only trying to help."

- "I think this would be a great opportunity for young kids, not only to become educated on things that are not necessarily taught in schools, but also to learn how to use their voices and talk openly with others about things that make people slightly uncomfortable (especially at that age). This paves a great path for open communication later in life."

13

Your Call to Action

Sex-education groups like Girls' Group are impactful. The previous chapter described, through direct feedback from participants, the positive influence this model had on the lives of the girls in my group. And I feel confident that these young women will continue to feel the ripple effects of GG for years to come, based on comments that the girls and their parents have shared with me since GG concluded.

The need for information to reach your kids is real, and it is ubiquitous. Teens are hungry for information to help them navigate life in real time, information that serves them as they grow into young adults and beyond. Your kids have the right to receive factual, developmentally appropriate sex-ed information in an environment where they feel safe, acknowledged, and empowered. Girls' Group addressed this at a micro level.

And this is where you have the chance to make a difference. What can you do so your kids have everything they need to make healthy choices throughout their lives? You are in a unique position, as a trusted adult in their lives, to repeat what worked for you when you were growing up or rewrite the template if it did not give you the useful info you wish you had when you were an adolescent.

Throughout this book, I have highlighted that, regardless of your upbringing and how you learned (or did not learn) about sex and all the connected topics, you can give your kids what is their birthright. The fact that you are reading this book is a wonderful indication that you are not only curious, you are ready. You are invested in your kids and understand that you have all that you need to take the next steps. What will be your first step?

Remember, you are never alone. Millions of parents are in the same boat of wanting to take steps forward. Consider partnering with a close friend or group of friends in making a commitment to positive changes in sex education, at a personal level with your kids and in the larger landscape in your community. Partnering helps keep you accountable, and also, it can be more fun.

PARENTAL CHALLENGE: Taking Your Next Step

Now that you have read about the informal modes of sex "education" that are reaching your child, reviewed the steps to assess and improve upon the formal education your child receives (including how to overcome your own heebie-jee-bies), and been given a blueprint for creating a sex-education group, what's next? To help you decide what your next steps are, you have one last Parental Challenge:

Based on all that you have learned about the variability of sex education in schools and kids' access to reliable information, what is your wish for your child?

Why is this important to you?

What role will you play in making it happen?

What is a first step to move you in that direction?

By when will you take that first step?

Who can you bring on board to keep you on track? Or even better, who will you partner with as accountability and motivational partners?

Congratulations! You are well on your way to more open, comfortable sex talks with your children. The steps shared with you in this book are simply tools that enable you to move past what was preventing you from being the communicator you want to be. With your heightened awareness for what prevented you from moving forward as a sex educator, you can be intentional in HOW (being yourself) and WHEN (at moments that feel right to you throughout your child's life) you put your knowledge to use. And once you do, you will find it's easier than you thought.

Sex and HIV Education Requirements in the United States per the Guttmacher Institute

General Requirements for Sex* and HIV Education

State	Sex education mandated	HIV education mandated	When provided, sex or HIV education must				Parental Role		
			Be medically accurate	Be age appropriate	Be culturally appropriate and unbiased	Cannot promote religion	Notice	Consent	Opt-out allowed
AL		X		X					X
AK							X		X
AZ			HIV	X			X	Sex	HIV
AR		X							
CA	X	X	X	X	X	X	X		X
CO			X	X	X	X	X		X
CT		X							X
DE	X	X							
DC	X	X		X			X		X
FL	X	X		X					X
GA	X	X					X		X
HI	X	X	X	X					X
ID									X
IL		X	X	X					X
IN		X					X		X
IA	X	X	X	X	X		X		X
KS	X								
KY	X	X							
LA			X			X			X
ME	X	X	X	X					X
MD	X	X					X		
MA					X		X		X
MI		X					X		X

216

State	Sex education mandated	HIV education mandated	When provided, sex or HIV education must				Parental Role		
			Be medically accurate	Be age appropriate	Be culturally appropriate and unbiased	Cannot promote religion	Notice	Consent	Opt-out allowed
MN	X	X							
MS	X			X			X	X	
MO		X	X	X			X		X
MT	X	X		X					X
NV	X	X		X			X	X	
NH	X	X					X		X
NJ	X	X	X	X	X		X		X
NM	X	X		X					X
NY		X		HIV					HIV
NC	X	X	X	X					X
ND	X	X							
OH	X	X							X
OK		X	HIV				X		X
OR	X	X	X	X	X		X		X
PA		X		HIV			HIV		HIV
RI	X	X	X	X	X				HIV
SC	X	X		X			X		X
TN		X	X	X	X		X	X	
TX	X	X		X			X		X
UT	X	X	X				X	X	
VT	X	X		X					HIV
VA	X	X	X	X			X		X
WA	X	X	X	X	X		X		X
WV	X	X							X
WI		X					X		X
Total	30+DC	39+DC	18	26+DC	9	3	25+DC	5	37+DC

Copied with permission from Guttmacher Institute

Content Requirements for Sex and HIV Education

State	When provided, sex education must include					When provided, HIV education must include	
	Contracep-tion	Abstinence	Importance of sex only within marriage	Sexual Orientation	Negative outcomes of teen sex	Condoms	Abstinence
Alabama	X	Stress	X	Negative		X	Stress
Arizona		Stress		Negative	X		Stress
Arkansas		Stress	X				Stress
California	X	Cover		Inclusive		X	Cover
Colorado	X	Stress		Inclusive	X	X	Cover
Conneticut	X	Cover		Inclusive	X		
Delaware	X	Stress		Inclusive		X	Stress
DC	X	Cover		Inclusive	X		Cover
Florida		Stress	X	Negative	X		Stress
Georgia		Stress	X				Cover
Hawaii	X	Stress				X	Stress
Idaho		Stress					
Illinois	X	Stress	X	Negative	X	X	Stress
Indiana		Stress	X		X		Stress
Iowa				Inclusive			
Kentucky		Stress					
Louisiana		Stress	X				Stress
Maine	X	Stress				X	Stress
Maryland	X	Cover		Inclusive		X	Cover
Michigan		Stress	X				Stress
Minnesota							Cover
Mississippi		Stress	X		X		Stress

State	When provided, sex education must include					When provided, HIV education must include	
	Contracep-tion	Abstinence	Importance of sex only within marriage	Sexual Orientation	Negative outcomes of teen sex	Condoms	Abstinence
Missouri		Stress	X		X		Stress
New Hampshire		Cover					Cover
New Jersey	X	Stress		Inclusive	X	X	Stress
New Mexico	X	Cover		Inclusive	X	X	Stress
New York							Stress
North Carolina	X	Stress	X		X	X	Stress
North Dakota		Cover	X		X		
Ohio		Stress	X		X		Stress
Oklahoma		Stress		X		X	Stress
Oregon	X	Stress		Inclusive		X	Stress
Pennsylvania							Stress
Rhode Island	X	Stress		Inclusive	X	X	Stress
South Carolina	X	Stress	X	Negative			Stress
South Dakota		Cover					
Tennessee		Stress	X		X		Stress
Texas	X	Stress	X	Negative	X	X	Stress
Utah		Stress	X				Stress
Vermont	X	Cover			X	X	Cover
Virginia	X	Cover	X		X	X	Cover
Washington	X	Stress		Inclusive		X	Stress
West Virginia	X	Cover			X	X	Cover
Wisconsin		Stress	X				Stress
TOTAL	20+DC	39+DC	19	16+DC	19+DC	19	37+DC

Sex Education* to Include Life Skills on Sexual Consent, Relationships and Prevention of Violence

State	Healthy relationships	Sexual decision-making and self-discipline	Refusal skills and personal boundaries	Consent	Dating and sexual violence prevention
Alabama		X	X		X
Alaska					X
Arizona	X	X	X		X
Arkansas	X	X	X		X
California	X	X	X	X	X
Colorado	X	X	X	X	X
Connecticut	X	X			X
Delaware	X	X	X	X	X
Dist. of Columbia	X	X	X	X	X
Florida	X	X			X
Georgia			X		X
Hawaii	X	X			
Idaho	X	X			
Illinois	X		X	X	X
Indiana					X
Iowa	X				X
Kentucky	X	X			
Louisiana	X	X			X
Maine	X	X			X
Maryland	X	X	X	X	X
Massachusetts	X				X
Michigan		X	X		X

State	Healthy relationships	Sexual decision-making and self-discipline	Refusal skills and personal boundaries	Consent	Dating and sexual violence prevention
Mississippi					X
Missouri		X	X		X
Nebraska	X				X
Nevada		X			
New Hampshire					X
New Jersey	X		X	X	X
New Mexico	X	X	X		X
North Carolina	X	X	X		X
Ohio	X				X
Oklahoma			X		
Oregon	X	X	X	X	X
Pennsylvania	X				
Rhode Island	X	X	X		X
South Carolina	X		X	X	X
Tennessee	X	X	X		X
Texas	X	X	X		X
Utah			X		X
Vermont	X	X			X
Virginia	X	X	X		X
Washington	X	X	X	X	X
West Virginia	X		X		X
Wisconsin					X
TOTAL	**31+DC**	**26+DC**	**24+DC**	**9+DC**	**37+DC**

*Sex education typically includes discussion of STIs

Resources

There are many wonderful sources of good information out there, as well as some that are less savory. Here I offer an abridged list of some of my favorites. I encourage you to search for additional resources that meet your needs.

Suggested Websites and Online Resources

Advocates for Youth (www.advocatesforyouth.org)
This group is committed to helping young people in their fight for sexual health, rights, and justice and has a plethora of tools available.

Amaze (for Parents) (www.amaze.org/parents/)
Sex-education information that helps parents talk with their kids factually in an age-appropriate manner.

Common Sense Media (www.commonsensemedia.org)
A valuable resource that enables parents to find ratings of appropriateness for books, movies, television, games, etc. simply by typing in the title of whatever it is they want to review.

Confi (www.confi.co)
An online resource, with expert-approved infographics, that addresses sexuality, reproductive health, mental health, and healthy relationships in a relatable and easy-to-digest format.

Gay, Lesbian, and Straight Education Network (www.glsen.org)
A national organization dedicated to ensuring that LGBTQ+ students have a safe and supportive learning environment free from bullying and harassment.

Gender Spectrum (www.genderspectrum.org)
A rich resource that creates gender-inclusive spaces throughout the primary domains of children's and teens' lives.

Go Ask Alice (www.goaskalice.columbia.edu/)
A comprehensive online health resource with extensive information on a variety of health topics including sexual and reproductive health.

Guttmacher Institute (www.guttmacher.org)
A research and policy organization focused on advancing sexual and reproductive rights of all people.

Our Bodies, Ourselves (www.ourbodiesourselves.org)
This online resource grew out of the book of the same name

that originated in the 1970s and later became an influential international sensation. It includes a plethora of information about women's bodies, health, sexuality, and so much more.

Parents, Families, and Friends of Lesbians and Gays (www.pflag.org)
PFLAG promotes the health and well-being of LGBTQ+ people and their families, friends, and allies through support, education, and advocacy.

Planned Parenthood (www.plannedparenthood.org/learn)
A wealth of information available to parents and teens, organized by topics and appropriate age groups, delivered in a respectful, nonjudgmental manner.

Scarleteen (www.scarleteen.com)
Comprehensive sex-education resource for teens.

Sex Positive Families (www.sexpositivefamilies.com)
Resource to help families raise sexually healthy children.

SIECUS (www.siecus.org)
Advocacy group with extensive resources to help promote comprehensive sex education for all.

Books

Books for Parents

- *Sex, Teens, & Everything in Between* by Shafia Zaloom

- *The Straight Talk on Parenting: A No-Nonsense Approach on How to Grow a Grown-Up* by Vicki Hoefle

- *Talk to Me First: Everything You Need to Know to Become Your Kids' "Go-To" Person about Sex* by Deborah Roffman

- *Sexploitation: Helping Kids Develop Healthy Sexuality in a Porn-Driven World* by Cindy Pierce

Books for Children

- *These Are My Eyes, This Is My Nose, This Is My Vulva, These Are My Toes* by Lexx Brown James

- *What Makes a Baby* by Cory Silverberg

- *It's Not the Stork!* by Robie H. Harris

- *It's So Amazing!* by Robie H. Harris

- *It's Perfectly Normal* by Robie H. Harris

- *C Is for Consent* by Eleanor Morrison

- *Sex Is a Funny Word* by Cory Silverberg

- *Will Puberty Last My Whole Life?* by Julie Metzger

- *Your Whole Body* by Lizzie DeYoung Charbonneau

Books for Teens

- *Changing Bodies, Changing Lives* by Ruth Bell
- *Our Bodies, Ourselves* by Boston Women's Health Book Collective
- *S.E.X.: The All-You-Need-to-Know Progressive Sexuality Guide to Get You through High School and College* by Heather Corinna

Young Adult Novels That Address Consent, Sex, Pregnancy, and Related Topics

- *Finding Yvonne* by Brandy Colbert
- *The Birds, the Bees, and You and Me* by Olivia Hinebaugh
- *Forever* by Judy Blume
- *When Dimple Met Rishi* by Sandhya Menon
- *Eleanor & Park* by Rainbow Rowell
- *Annie on My Mind* by Nancy Garden
- *Aristotle and Dante Discover the Secrets of the Universe* by Benjamin Alire Sáenz
- *I Wish You All the Best* by Mason Deaver

Examples of Evidence-Based and Evidence-Informed Curricula

The curricula listed here cover an array of topics for a broad range of audience ages as specified. The programs included in this abridged list were created with a school-based, community-based, or web-based setting in mind, where indicated. However, there is flexibility in how the majority of them can be adapted. Some require training or professional development, while others do not. Similarly, some require fees, while others are available free of charge. I encourage you to explore these as well as others you find to determine what best fits your needs.

Becoming a Responsible Teen (BART): community based; ages 14–18; 8 lessons

Draw the Line/Respect the Line: school based; ages 12–14; 19 lessons

Get Real: Comprehensive Sex Education That Works: school based; ages 12–18; 38 lessons

FOCUS: Preventing STIs and Unwanted Pregnancies among Young Women: community based; ages 16+; 4 lessons

Family Life and Sexual Health (FLASH): school based; ages 9–18; 50 lessons

It's Your Game . . . Keep It Real! (IYG): school based; ages 12–14; 24 lessons

Making Proud Choices!: community based; ages 12–18; 8–10 lessons

Michigan Model for Health: school based; ages 9–18; 34 lessons

My Future, My Choice: school based; ages 12–14; 10 lessons

Native It's Your Game: web based; ages 12–14; 13 lessons

Nu-CULTURE: school based; ages 12–14; 24 lessons

Our Whole Lives (OWL): community based; ages 5–18; 57 lessons

Positive Prevention Plus: school based; ages 9–18; 33 lessons

Reducing the Risk: school based; ages 14–18; 16 lessons

Rights, Respect, Responsibility (3Rs): school based; ages 5–18; 78 lessons

Safer Choices: school based; ages 14–18; 21 lessons

Sexuality Education for People with Developmental Disabilities: school/community based; ages 14+; 22 lessons

Icebreakers

Toilet Paper Roll

Pass around a roll of toilet paper and ask participants to "take what you need." After the roll has made its way to everyone, ask each participant to say one thing about themselves for each square of toilet paper they have, starting with their name.

Benefit: this gets people talking about themselves.

What If

This icebreaker allows you to be as creative as you like with the questions you ask your participants. Have them write down their answers to different "What if" scenarios and go around reading their responses. Examples include (1) If you had one superpower, what would it be?, (2) If you could go back in time, when would you travel to?, and (3) If you had one adjective floating about your head, what would it be?

Benefit: the sky is the limit in what questions you ask and what participants can learn about each other.

Fact vs. Fiction

Have each person take an index card and write two truths about themselves that may not be known to others, as well as one lie. Go around the table and have them read their three items in a random order while the others guess which are fact and which are fiction.

Benefit: This game helps people get to know each other and learn things they would not have otherwise known. It also is a good example of how some things can sound believable but are not truth.

Name Chain

Go around the table having each participant state their name and a sex-education word that begins with the same letter as their name. Example: "My name is Beth, and my word is breast." Then, the next person has to restate the previous participant's name and word before introducing themselves. Example: "Hi, Beth whose word is breast. I am Ella, and my word is erection."

Benefit: this game gets people to learn one another's names and become more comfortable using sex-education terminology.

Condom Catch

Fill a condom with some water and tie it closed so it can be used as a ball. Throw it to a group participant who has to say a sexual-health word that begins with the letter A before throwing it to another participant who has to say a sexual-health word that begins with B, and so on. This continues until the alphabet is complete.

Benefit: this game gets people having fun with sexual-health vocabulary and is an opportunity to demonstrate how robust and safe condoms are.

References

Chapter 1: Facts about Sex Education in the United States

1. "About Teen Pregnancy," Centers for Disease Control and Prevention, accessed February 19, 2021, www.cdc.gov/teenpregnancy/about/index.htm#.

2. "STDs in Young Adults and Adolescents," Centers for Disease Control and Prevention, accessed April 15, 2020, www.cdc.gov/std/stats17/adolescents.htm#.

3. "The SIECUS State Profiles," Sexual Information and Education Council of the United States, accessed February 19, 2021, siecus.org/state-profiles/.

4. Mandy A. Allison, Laura P. Hurley, Lauri Markowitz, Lori A. Crane, Michaela Brtnikova, Brenda L. Beaty, Megan Snow, Janine Cory, Shannon Stokley, Jill Roark, and Allison Kempe, "Primary Care Physicians' Perspectives About HPV Vaccine," *Pediatrics* 137, no. 2 (February 2016): doi.org/10.1542/peds.2015-2488.

Chapter 2: Sexual Content Is Everywhere

5. "The Prevalence of Porn," PsychCentral, accessed February 19, 2020, psychcentral.com/blog/sex/2013/05/the-prevalence-of-porn#1.

6. "The Stats of Internet Pornography," The D Info-

graphics, accessed February 19, 2021, thedinfographics
.com/2011/12/23/internet-pornography-statistics/.

7. "An Ode to Fabio, Romance Model King," Bookstr, accessed March 1, 2021, bookstr.com/article/an-ode-to-fabio-romance-novel-king/.

8. "About the Romance Genre," Romance Writers of America, accessed February 19, 2021, www.rwa.org/Online/Romance_Genre/About_Romance_Genre.aspx.

9. "'Fifty Shades of Grey' Was the Best-Selling Book of the Decade in the US, The NPD Group Says," The NPD Group, Inc., accessed July 3, 2020, www.npd.com/wps/portal/npd/us/news/press-releases/2019/fifty-shades-of-grey-was-the-best-selling-book-of-the-decade-in-the-u-s-the-npd-group-says/.

Chapter 3: The Need for Comprehensive Sex Ed for Kids

10. "Why Does Sex-Ed matter? Because science says so!" Action Canada for Sexual Health & Rights, accessed August 17, 2020, www.actioncanadashr.org/resources/sexual-health-info/sex-ed/why-does-sex-ed-matter-because-science-says-so.

11. WHO Recommendations on Adolescent Sexual and Reproductive Health and Rights (Geneva: World Health Organization, 2018).

12. "'No Promo Homo' Laws," GLSEN, accessed April 6, 2020, www.glsen.org/activity/no-promo-homo-laws.

13. "Sexual Abuse of People With I/DD a Global Scandal," *The Arc*, posted November 19, 2013, thearc.org/sexual-abuse-people-idd-global-scandal/.

14. Mia Barrett, "Acknowledging Pleasure in Sexuality Education," *ETR*, posted December 19, 2019, www.etr.org/blog/acknowledging-pleasure-in-sexuality-education/.

Chapter 4: Get Involved in Your Child's Sex Education

15. Janis Wolak, Kimberly Mitchell, and David Finkelhor, "Unwanted and Wanted Exposure to Online Pornography in a National Sample of Youth Internet Users," *Pediatrics* 119, no. 2 (February 2007): 247–57, doi.org/10.1542/peds.2006-1891.

16. Chiara Sabina, Janis Wolak, and David Finkelhor, "The Nature and Dynamics of Internet Pornography Exposure for Youth," *CyberPsychology & Behavior* 11, no. 6 (December 2008), doi.org/10.1089/cpb.2007.0179.

Chapter 6: Step 2—Determine Which Sex-Ed Topics Are Taught in School

17. "On Our Side: Public Support for Sex Education," Sexuality Education and Information Council of the United States, last updated August 2018, siecus.org/wp-content/

uploads/2018/08/On-Our-Side-Public-Support-for-Sex-Ed-2018-Final.pdf.

18. Guttmacher Institute, "Sex and HIV Education," State Law and Policies (as of March 1, 2021), New York: Guttmacher Institute, 2021, www.guttmacher.org/state-policy/explore/sex-and-hiv-education#.

Chapter 7: Step 3—Consider Community Resources

19. Stewart C. Alexander, J. Dennis Fortenberry, Kathryn I. Pollak, Terrill Bravender, J. Kelly Davis, Truls Østbye, James A. Tulsky, Rowena J. Dolor, and Cleveland G. Shields, "Sexuality Talk During Adolescent Health Maintenance Visits," *JAMA Pediatrics* 168, no. 2 (February 2014): 163–169, doi.org/10.1001/jamapediatrics.2013.4338.

20. Cora C. Breuner and Gerri Mattson, "Sexuality Education for Children and Adolescents," *Pediatrics* 138, no. 2 (August 2016), doi.org/10.1542/peds.2016-1348.

About the Author

Andrea Brand is a passionate proponent of comprehensive sex education and helping parents embrace their role as open, trusty resources for their kids.

Her work as a life coach focuses on supporting women interested in trading in feelings of overwhelm for confidence and contentment. She worked for decades in public health, initially in direct care and then as a research consultant to impact programs and policy. After exploring her own inner conflict that resulted from the competing demands of a fast-paced corporate culture and life outside of the office, she stepped away from her career to evaluate her priorities and focus on what matters most to her: family, interpersonal connections, and living authentically. This led to her work connected to sex education as well as helping others live more purposefully.

Andrea holds MSW and MPH degrees from the University of Michigan. Now an empty nester, she resides in Massachusetts with her husband and dog.

ARB Coaching, LLC
www.arbcoaching.com
Available for speaking, coaching, and consulting